BAR INTERNATIONAL SERIES 3091 | 2022

3D Surveying Methods and Digital Information Management for Archaeological Heritage

ANGELA BOSCO

Published in 2022 by
BAR Publishing, Oxford, UK

BAR International Series 3091

*3D Surveying Methods and Digital Information Management
for Archaeological Heritage*

ISBN 978 1 4073 5973 1 paperback
ISBN 978 1 4073 5974 8 e-format

DOI https://doi.org/10.30861/9781407359731

A catalogue record for this book is available from the British Library

COVER IMAGE *Foreground image – section of a 3D laser scanner point cloud of the
Roman maritime villa of Villa Sora in Torre del Greco. Background image – 3D survey
with terrestrial photogrammetry of the Collegio degli Augustali in Herculaneum.*

BAR titles are available from:

BAR Publishing
122 Banbury Rd, Oxford, OX2 7BP, UK
info@barpublishing.com
www.barpublishing.com

Of Related Interest

3D and 4D Cartography of Archaeological Stratigraphy
A case study at the Western Forum in Ostia Antica
Undine Lieberwirth
BAR International Series **3040** | 2021

Antro delle gallerie, indagini di archeologia mineraria in Valganna (Varese)
Amedeo Gambini
BAR International Series **2916** | 2019

Tecniche di rilevamento e metodi di rappresentazione per l'Architettura Rupestre
Il Monastero Benedettino di Subiaco
Andrea Angelini
BAR International Series **2889** | 2018

Making Visible: Three-dimensional GIS in Archaeological Excavation
Stefania Merlo
BAR International Series **2801** | 2016

3D Recording and Modelling in Archaeology and Cultural Heritage
Theory and best practices
Fabio Remondino and Stefano Campana
BAR International Series **2598** | 2014

Beyond Illustration: 2D and 3D Digital Technologies as Tools for Discovery in Archaeology
Bernard Frischer and Anastasia Dakouri-Hild
BAR International Series **1805** | 2008

Non basta guardare,
occorre guardare con occhi che vogliono vedere,
che credono in quello che vedono.
(Galileo Galilei)

A Sofia e Simone

Acknowledgements

This book would not have been possible without the work of the CISA research team. I would therefore like to thank my colleagues and friends: Andrea D'Andrea, Rosario Valentini, Francesca Forte, Laura Carpentiero, Eleonora Minucci, Marco Barbarino, Gilda Ferrandino and the presidents Prof. Bruno Genito and Prof. Roberta Giunta.

I would also like to thank Prof. Fabrizio Pesando, who 'adopted' me at a time that was not easy, and to dedicate an affectionate memory to Prof. Gianni Bailo Modesti, who left a deep mark on my academic life.

A heartfelt thank you to the directors of the Archaeological Parks of Pompeii and Herculaneum, who have succeeded each other in these years of research: Massimo Osanna, Gabriel Zuchtriegel, Maria Paola Guidobaldi and Francesco Sirano.

I would like to thank the members of the research team for the Solar Temple of Abusir project: Rosanna Pirelli, Massimiliano Nuzzolo, Emanuele Brienza and Patrizia Zanfagna; the whole group of the beautiful project "Ancient Appia Landscapes" and in particular Alfonso Santoriello and the working group of the S. Biagio alla Venella project: Teresa Cinquantaquattro, Carlo Rescigno, Angela Pontrandolfo, Luca Cerchiai and Fausto Longo.

I cannot fail to thank my beautiful family: my parents Lilli and Antonio, my brother Roberto, Sofia, Emilio, Francesco and Ana. In particular thanks to my husband Antonio, without whom I would not have been able to do this, and to my children Sofia and Simone, constant sources of inspiration, endless sources of love.

We are grateful to the anonymous referees for their valuable comments and suggestions.

Contents

List of Figures

Preface

Talking about digital tools in archaeology may still seem a trivial and outdated topic. Computer technology with sophisticated techniques and algorithms pervades every field of human activity and, therefore, also of archaeological research. Despite of this, there are still some scholars who are intolerant, if not reluctant, to admit that every step we take is marked using the computer or by its digitization in a world crowded with bits. We speak of digital born data, digital natives and today, after the COVID19 epidemic, digital nomads. The adjective digital is not perceived as an alternative or contrary to analogue; it is part of our way of being citizens of a universe in which information travels at a speed that was unimaginable before.

Is it all roses and flowers, the scenario that lies ahead for us as inhabitants of the world and researchers? Even if we were completely contrary, we cannot stop or slow down a process of transformation that invests, like an avalanche, everything that meets on its path. Shadows and lights intertwine, and will increasingly intertwine, in our being digital – as predicted by Nicholas Negroponte back in 1995 – in our daily lives as in our professional and academic careers.

Long clarifications in scientific papers and talks at international conferences on what GIS and SfM algorithm are and how they work, or which is the best pipeline for the use of a software, widely used, such as Metashape is not useful today. These were already discussed over ten years ago, and perhaps a reminder of some pioneering work or recent surveys would not hurt. The world of digital archaeology often suffers from temporary amnesia, easy falling in love, escapes into the future and, above all, spectacularism.

As happened in the more or less recent past, the digital tools used in archaeological research derive from technological conceptual developments that come from other domains whose frontiers are often characterized by multi and interdisciplinary approaches. The genius of some researchers lies in their ability to bring seemingly complex technological transformations to the field of historical research, encouraging methodological reflections that end up changing or positively conditioning the professional action of the archaeologist. Too many colleagues, especially young ones, seem more focused on the development of specific software for archaeology than interested in questioning the outcomes that technologies produce in research.

Often code or uncritical use of the tool replaces an attitude, which should be natural in research, to understanding the processes identified and implemented and the countless facets that new data impose on our way of reasoning. Today, digital research should rather dedicate itself to the analysis of relationships, for example GIS-BIM, to the deepening of the forms of integration of 3D technologies, highlighting, in particular, the problems related to the accuracy and geometric precision of surveys, to the development of new forms of registration and management of archives to ensure the sharing of data and their accessibility and, finally, to the creation of archaeological libraries and/or thesauri.

The merit of Angela Bosco, with her book, is to have brought the theme of digital archaeology in an area of reflection and critical discussion outside of the prevailing strong exaltation of the bit and coding. In the short introductory chapter, the author illustrates the technologies used in her work in the field, extending the discussion to the most recent BIM and the methods of recording. Subsequently, Angela Bosco offers the reader some case studies referring to different contexts and – aspect of great scientific interest – to different fields of use, trying to grasp the connection between tools and final results.

Fortunately, the book does not exalt the confidence in the progress of scientific knowledge that permeates too many contributions focused on the use of information technology and digital tools in Archaeology. The reader, on the contrary, will find constant references to the research questions, to the investigations in the field and, in conclusion, to the scientific results that are, we must always remember, the final objective of our work.

Andrea D'Andrea

Overview

After a brief introduction summarizing the objectives of the activities conducted in recent years by the author, the first chapter analyses the 3D survey methods mostly used in the field of cultural heritage and increasingly in demand in archaeology. These are i) the terrestrial and aerial SfM (Structure from Motion) photogrammetry, and ii) the laser scanner survey method.

Photogrammetry is widely used due to low software and equipment costs. It allows one to obtain a 3D textured model with a mesh and to easily extract high resolution ortho-photos of the relevant surfaces, on which to perform the stratigraphic study or analysis of degradation. However, a good topographic support with GPS or the Total Station is necessary to obtain reliable metric results.

The laser scanner methods, on the other hand, are certainly more expensive, both for the equipment and the dedicated software. However, they allow, for the immediate production of metric point clouds down to the millimetre and including RGB information. This is because the most advanced lasers may acquire 360-degrees panoramic photos that can then be used to extrapolate relevant information on the colours that in turn match with the points. However, the resolution of such photos is not optimal. Only rarely then one can extract accurate information (i.e. down to the centimetre) – especially when it comes to wall painted decorations, frescoes or some degradation phenomena. For these it is often necessary to make a follow-up (high resolution) photo shoot.

In the same chapter we then illustrate how the metadata evolved with the advent of the 'digital born' data. Doing so, we may identify the most suitable schemes for storing three-dimensional information, capable of keeping track the motivations (paradata) and the tools (provenance) behind the survey. We then discuss the possible ways to manage the large amount of information obtained as result of their elaboration.

The management of 3D data is at the centre of the academic debate. Archaeologists largely use GIS (Geographical Information System), as this enables complex analysis based on the integration of geographic and alphanumeric data. For this reason, the GIS system has been further developed by adapting recent 3D technique developments. However, this is only limited to a visual implementation. This is because the information can be mapped into 3D only through a vectorization that is still bi-dimensional.

Another system known as BIM (Building Information Modelling) is increasingly used for HBIM (Historical Building Information Modelling) purposes. This was introduced for the first time in the construction industry – in order to manage all the different life-cycles of a building, from planning to demolition. BIM is based on parametric models that allow the matching of different types of information (e.g., numeric databases, images and geographic information) to the 3D object at hand. However, BIM software was not been developed for historical artifacts. As a consequence, existing libraries are only relevant to modern buildings. There is then a need to integrate libraries with information tailored to historic buildings.

This contribution intends to analyse in detail the methods and the potential developments in this 3D survey space, with reference to the different areas of archaeological research.

The second chapter focuses on applications related to on field archaeological research works. Probably what is really striking about the application of 3D in archaeology is that these techniques allow the possibility of re-experiencing and 'reliving' the – inevitably destructive – excavation phase, even long after its execution. This is because by associating the 3D acquisition with the most classic excavation documentation one can keep replicas of the layers with their visual, metric and volumetric information. This at any time allows their virtual consultation, in all their stratigraphic relationships and without subjective interpretations.

We will present two applications of these techniques in the context of the projects of 'San Biagio alla Venella' (Metaponto) in 2015 and 'Ancient Appia Landscapes' (Benevento) in 2016. For these, the documentation work related to the stratigraphic trenches, goes alongside the contextualization in the surrounding landscape and is augmented with information from previous research.

In the 'Sanctuary of S. Biagio' project, old and new excavations are matched following the digitization of all the data collected to date. A series of laser scans, then, allow the digital visualization of the modern landscape providing the basis for the reconstruction of the ancient one.

The objective of the 'Ancient Appia Landscapes' (AAL) project, is the study of the Appian Way in the *Beneventum* territory and the identification of those socio-economic phenomena that led to the developments of settlement along with this fundamental road axis.

All information, whether archived or from surveys and excavations, is managed *via* a GIS information system. The 'topographical units' are systematically surveyed via GPS. The excavation documentation is managed in the same way. In the 2016 intervention area (i.e. in the surroundings of 'Masseria Grasso'), where traces of a productive area were found, some surveys were programmed using SfM photogrammetry.

In the third chapter we analyse the needs for the enhancement of an archaeological site. This is crucial for an adequate conservation and maintenance project and represents an essential starting point to plan an adequate public use of the site.

To this end, the 'Villa Sora' project was started in Torre del Greco. The Roman maritime villa in the Sora district has a long and troubled history. It was first explored in 1797, and examined in different periods by many archaeologists and architects. It was damaged by the passage of the Naples-Sorrento railway line in the mid-1800s and by the expansion of the local cemetery. It is also located in an area not easy to access, exclusively connected by a rather bumpy country road. The project involved the survey of the entire archaeological area with laser scanner and photogrammetry.

After processing the 3D data, the digital replica was cleaned out of all modern elements (i.e., the metal coverage of the area with decorated and paved rooms, the plinths supporting the cladding, the surrounding fence and the railway). This provided an overview of the original and still existing buildings and the related archaeological levels. To ensure an appropriate understanding of the site, all the historical surveys, which retain information on what has been destroyed over time, have been digitized and compared with each other and with the relief obtained from 3D. This way a number of inconsistencies became visible. Starting from 3D data and from the analysis of the walls of the villa destroyed by the Vesuvius in 79 AD, two different virtual reconstructions are proposed. This represented the basis for the virtual restoration of the villa.

For the so-called '*Augusteum*' of Herculaneum researchers have focused on the enhancement of a building that for the most part is still buried under the debris of the 79 AD eruption. An accurate three-dimensional survey of the exposed architectonic structures was therefore planned (the four-faced arch of the south corner of the portico). The analysis of the floor plans obtained in the Bourbon period (with the use of tunnels), and the review of recent functional reinterpretation of the building, allowed to draw basic vector information, which, in turn, enabled a virtual reconstruction of the building. The two reliefs were then compared to refine the reconstructive model.

Some furnishing (i.e., statues and paintings currently part of the National Archaeological Museum of Naples collection) was virtually relocated. The statues were acquired by using SfM photogrammetry technique in order to obtain digital duplications, absolutely identical to the originals. The models so obtained were included,

within the 3DICONS project, within the European online library and are available to the general public in reduced and full format – available to scholars on request.

In the chapter four we will talk about conservation, a topic at the centre of scientific debate in recent past, particularly following the catastrophic events that have affected Pompeii and which have led to the conservation intervention known as the 'Great Pompeii Project'. The starting point for this intervention plan was the concept of preventive maintenance, impossible to implement without adequate documentation on the actual conditions of the buildings. Another plan of this Pompeian project, known as the 'Knowledge Plan', was also intended to take steps in this direction. This also made use – in selected areas – of surveys based on tools for three-dimensional acquisition.

Even prior to the implementation of such an extraordinary project, different acquisition methods for the restitution of three-dimensional data had already been used for the case studies of the '*domus* of Eros Stallius' (I, 6, 13-14) and *domus* of '*Centauro*' (VI, 9, 3- 5) in Pompeii. These were aimed at creating an accurate survey and supports for the analysis of the degradation of the architectonic structures. Low-cost terrestrial and aerial photogrammetric survey techniques had been tested, so as to obtain a total coverage of all the rooms of the house (including walls, roofs and 360-degrees view including the road network and the adjacent houses) This was performed at such a resolution in order to allow one to observe both structural and surface degradation.

The integration of these surveys turned out to be an adequate system both for the documentation objectives, and to verify the accuracy of the survey, including degradations of the upper floors of the buildings. This was possible despite the fact that the two surveys presented very different photographic resolutions also due the difficult conditions in which the surveys had taken place. This is because the acquisitions with drone were only possible in the very early hours of the morning, when the site is not accessible to tourists, with unfavourable light conditions. In addition, some rooms were so narrow and dark that even (i.e. ground) shooting was difficult.

Fifth chapter is deep-dive into the Archaeological Building Information Modelling (ABIM). This is an innovative management system of three-dimensional data from archaeological contexts, derivation of HBIM. The application of BIM in archaeology responds to the need to manage a large set of varied data, starting from the three-dimensional model of ancient buildings, to systematize and make these available to multiple professional figures. BIM modelling software can rely on libraries of objects. These allow the reproduction of building materials, machinery used for production plants furnishings that manufactures actually produce. Requisite to apply BIM is the availability of 'families' of objects with characteristics close to the reality, both in terms of structure and materials. To date there are no libraries dedicated to archaeological objects, but some recent scientific contributions offer suggestions as to how to systematically create such new taxonomies.

The activities at the 'Niuserra Solar Temple in Abu Ghurab' (Egypt), allowed to experiment such innovative management system on a number of archaeological information with different characteristics. The aim of the activity was to generate an accurate documentation of this important Egyptian site, in order to better understand its original structure. This required a multidisciplinary approach which involved, in addition to archaeologists, architects and structural engineers. The use of BIM has, then, allowed people from varied professional backgrounds to access and draw on information within the same system, without loss of data while operating in three dimensions.

Introduction

The present work is the result of research carried out from 2013 to 2018, in the framework of research projects carried out with the Università degli Studi di Napoli "L'Orientale" (i.e. International project 3D-ICONS, which saw as leading partner CISA – Centro Interdipartimentale di Servizi di Archeologia) and with the Dipartimento di Scienze del Patrimonio Culturale (DiSPaC) of the Università di Salerno, where the writer obtained her PhD degree.

The documentation process in the archaeological field has significantly improved thanks to the dissemination of technologically sophisticated investigation methods. Such technologies, already employed in commercial contexts, enable faster operations and unprecedented accuracy of representation.

Although, these new techniques offer ground-breaking opportunities for academic research, their full potential has not yet been exploited. This may be because, a simple 3D survey of a monument, even if extremely accurate, is not enough to obtain good scientific results.

Unfortunately, archaeologists are not always familiar with computer graphics innovations and rarely with Computational Archaeology. This results in a lack of systematization of methodological procedures and, in most cases, the accumulation of high-quality data is not fully exploited.

The collapses of archaeological areas in Pompeii and Rome have created great media clamour around the world. However, beyond the public outrage, they also highlighted the important need to develop new ways to protect Italian archaeological heritage

With this in mind, in 2011, the *Ministero dei Beni e delle Attività Culturali e del Turismo*, approved an extraordinary project, within the Great Pompeii Project (GPP)[1]. Its focus would have been the conservation and the enhancement of this archaeological area following a new methodology. which had been successfully tested in some other archaeological areas. It is the development of innovative methodologies that has inspired this work. In particular, as the methodology from the GPP project is now been inserted in the "Linee guida per la conservazione del patrimonio archeologico".

These guidelines which are examined by the *Consiglio Superiore dei beni culturali e paesaggistici* are based

on the innovative concept of "planned maintenance". Planned maintenance provides for systematic collection of information about assets and timely drafting adequate conservation plans.

The guidelines also touch on data collection through a project called "Knowledge Plan". The plan proposes arranging prior information in a single information system and integrating it with new (digital) data extracted from three-dimensional surveys. This new data is made with instruments capable of analytically documenting any type of monument, object or masonry.

The Knowledge Plan represents an innovative approach to the protection of cultural heritage. It enables the surveying of materials and structures' state of deterioration, while simultaneously collecting, archiving and managing the data. This approach is essential to better understand archaeological heritage, monitor how its state of conservation evolves and assess the sustainability and safety of maintenance plans.

This Knowledge Plan applies an innovative and expeditious surveying method, the three-dimensional digital survey, to heterogeneous information (e.g. identification and consistency of materials, surveys, studies, analysis results, archival documentation, previous interventions, etc.). This survey method is performed with laser-scanning or photogrammetric methods.

The 1972 Restoration Charter already defines a specific and widely tested procedure for the conservation and restoration of artistic assets, which often requires considerable investment (analysis, training of specialized workers, adaptation of scientific and non-scientific technical personnel). However, it has not yet clarified a unique methodology for the "knowledge" of artistic assets, to be understood as a systematic collection of documentation.

The Knowledge Plan, when implementing information gathering procedures, highlighted the importance and multiplicity of uses of three-dimensional surveying. However, it did not expand in detail regarding the various management issues.

Certainly, Pompeii represents a privileged site for the development of 3D acquisition methodologies. In recent years, the SIAV – Vesuvius Archaeological Information System and the "archaeological risk monitoring map 2010-2011" systems have been developed to monitor this archaeological site. However, although these systems propose two complementary approaches, they cannot

---

[1] Approved on 29 March 2012 by the European Community.

immediately dialogue with each other[2]. Another project worth mentioning on new interesting ideas for the arrangement of the data is the Herculaneum Conservation Project[3]. This project deals with the conservation of the nearby Vesuvian city of Herculaneum, which although smaller in scale is comparable to Pompeii in complexity[4].

The aim of this work is to suggest, through direct experimentation, 3D methodologies that satisfy the most common archaeological requests. I will be doing this by applying these methodologies to real cases that are representative of different research macro-topics. In particular, I will analyse (i) the potential of these innovative investigation methodologies and how critical they are, (ii) the difficulties of managing the data obtained (big data) and (iii) the interoperability with archaeological activities such as excavation, conservation and enhancement.

---

[2] Cinquantaquattro 2011
[3] http://www.herculaneum.org
[4] Thompson, D'Andrea 2009

Survey and Three-dimensional Data for Archaeology

The following sections will deal with innovative methodologies for three-dimensional survey in archaeology, by analysing specific techniques and types of application.

This type of discussion cannot disregard the fundamental principles of documentation in the archaeological field, which are based on the "ability to see" mentioned by Daniele Manacorda in the preface to Maura Medri's Handbook[1] of Archaeological Survey. The optimal condition for the purpose, expects that the surveyor is an archaeologist, which knows what he is documenting, understands the issues that the excavation, the structure and the site pose and knows the questions that the researcher wants to address.

Therefore, the survey has the dual function of both documentation and interpretation tool, which cannot be reduced to a merely technical process.

Over time, the surveyor archaeologist has adopted the methodologies of graphic representation developed in the field of architecture, constructing his own syntax, made up of a specific symbology and a greater graphic "freedom" that could meet the complexity of his own study contexts.

Taking a small step back, the interest in graphic representation in archaeology originated with growing curiosity, scientific advances, and the desire to contextualise the numerous remains of ancient monuments visible in 17th century Europe. At that time the antiquaries did not yet have a common graphic language, and the reliefs often represented structures in perspective and axonometry, with an artistic characterisation typical of the engravings of the time. Especially in the Anglo-Saxon context, the first planimetries appeared towards the end of the century, and they were perfected in the following century with the growing attention to archaeological excavation. The splendid plans of Herculaneum and Pompeii from the mid-18th century (Figure 1) are proof of the level of metric accuracy and also of graphic standardization that was achieved at that time, with sections marked in red, excavation limits smoothed out and rooms carefully numbered.

Representation methods were particularly refined in the Mediterranean, due to the great stratification and chronological complexity that characterises the sites, which therefore require specific technical expedients in plans and sections to define their phases. The 20th century saw a revolution in detailed stratigraphic restitution. In 1922 the sections of Wheeler's Segotium excavation were taken as an example of clarity in the transmission of information and, above all, of the scholar's interpretation. The Anglo-Saxon archaeological research that followed Wheeler's work, albeit in a personalised style, took it as a starting point and perfected it, adding, for example, graphic conventions to make the reading of the layers clearer and beginning to number the different features[2].

Subsequently, there has been a lot of innovation in the field of archaeological documentation. In addition to increasingly high-performance topographical instruments, a revolution occurred with the introduction of a practice that profoundly changed the operations of field surveyors: the photography. Indeed, when photography was systematically used on excavations, in the first decades of the 20th century, the most positivist spirits, eager to make the discipline a science with specific research objectives, pushed hard for photography to be imposed within the practices of archaeological documentation[3]. At the beginning, photography was considered supplant drawing as a far more objective medium, free of pre-interpretation, reporting reality as it appeared, in other words, a very different tool from drawing. But it is precisely this diversity that has meant that this "substitution" has not taken place. The two practices have, in a way, merged, becoming an indispensable part of the documentation process, together with filing and excavation journals.

Even if perfect, a photo will always have details that are not easy to interpret, such as small differences in level or slopes, which can be easily represented in excavation plans, despite they are two-dimensional, thanks to specific graphic indicators and the presence of dimensioned points.

Although the types of planimetric drawing carried out during an excavation are numerous and many of these differ from excavation to excavation and from nation to nation, they are all characterised by common elements that are indispensable for correct graphic restitution.

The need to document a destructive process such as that of archaeological excavation has made it essential to develop different "views" of the investigated area, which vary in detail from the plan of the single stratigraphic unit (SU), through the phase plan, to the composite plan that generally represents the end of the excavation.

---

[1] Medri 2003

[2] This is the case, among others, of the archaeologist Stuart Piggott, whose personal assessment of Wheeler's work was also commented on by Edward Harris, who called it an important transitional moment in the history of archaeological graphic representation (see Morgan, Wright 2018).

[3] Purche 2015

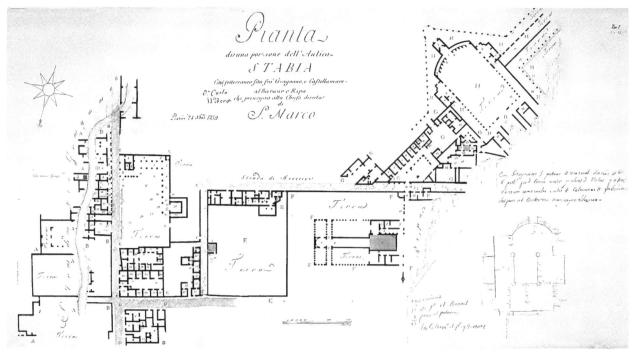

Figure 1. Plan of Villa S. Marco in Stabia. Carlo Weber 1759. (Credit: Ruggiero, Michele)

Through different surveying methods, the field archaeologist does not limit himself at documenting something that is disappearing; the drawing on site is the opportunity for reasoning. The excavation stops, everything is cleaned up, photos are taken; at that moment, he tries to define the stratigraphy, the relationships between the stratigraphic units, the actions that actually happened in that place. Interpretation is inevitable and inseparable from the practice of drawing. Without interpretation it would not be possible to distinguish and define features clearly, it would not be possible to assign a correct progressive number to stratigraphic units and consequently it would be more difficult to reconstruct historical events. Several theories formulated in this phase of acquisition on site may later be disproved by the analysis of the materials found in the strata or by bioarchaeological and archaeobotanical analyses. Nevertheless, the survey activity is of paramount importance in the practice of excavation and, therefore, in archaeological research.

Direct survey methods, still widely used in the field, are those (as the word itself suggests) that allow a 'physical' approach to the archaeological evidence. Hence, it would seem to be the most suitable methodology for the interpretative purpose of the archaeologist.

Actually, the advent of digital instruments – which we could now define as "traditional", such as GPS for global positioning and total stations – have not deeply changed the approach to archaeological representation, although they define the methodologies of indirect survey. In fact, it has been a technological upgrade that has made data acquisition operations more expeditious and, in many cases, more precise. On one hand, metric rollers,

plumb lines and optical theodolites have been replaced by technologically advanced instruments that perform trigonometric calculations in real time and allow the survey to be placed in a three-dimensional context. On the other hand, the method of restitution has not changed at all, keeping the same characteristics as pencil drawing on glossy paper, although it is mostly digital. The surveyor archaeologist still makes a selection and inevitably uses the filter of interpretation.

The unstoppable process of digitisation, which involves vectorialisation within specific drawing software, is a process that involves surveys that were conceived in analogical form. It is a transition indispensable to supply the numerous archaeological databases. In these cases, the drawing on paper is returned to the computer, sometimes with processes similar to ink polishing, i.e., by scanning the paper work and tracing the image after appropriate scaling, or by digitally reporting the trilateration operations similarly as preliminarily done with the compasses used on the sheet during the direct survey. These operations are often very time-consuming, at least as long as the original survey, and it is exactly to avoid this double step that the concept of digital acquisition has entered the world of archaeological documentation.

Therefore, the relationship with technology changes, and it becomes much more critical, when it comes to digital media, such as tablets and graphics tablets, and tools for three-dimensional data acquisition.

These tools are used in very different ways, often discontinuously, on multiple archaeological sites and excavations. Few research groups have so far succeeded in integrating these field-based digital acquisition methodologies with more traditional excavation documentation in a way that could be described as homogeneous. Among these is certainly the site of Çatalhöyük in Turkey. In this site, in 2009, 3D digital acquisition of every single phase of the excavation was applied on an experimental basis[4], using laser and photogrammetry tools.

This survey method was aimed at obtaining a three-dimensional stratigraphy that would be available at all times for the researchers on the field, who could virtually 'browse' through the different phases of excavation and observe in detail the characteristics of the different layers that have been removed. Researchers have found this approach extremely useful and beneficial to research, claiming that it is conducive to a reflective approach on the field. Therefore, this practice has been systematically used in different areas – with a specific acquisition plan pre-, during, and post-excavation – and combined with the use of tablets to make sketches from photographs and excavation notes.

By contrast to positive testimonies such as that of Çatalhöyük, there are diametrically opposed opinions, which see great risks in the use of such survey methods. While the Turkish site praises the ability of 3D to include multiple types of information and to generate new impulses for archaeological research, for many other scholars three-dimensional acquisition appears to be an indiscriminate assumption of data which, deprived of the reflective reasoning that is associated with the practice of drawing, can become an indistinct mass of information.

On numerous occasions, archaeology has shown that it is very open to innovation benefitting from it by converting to own needs the technological tools created for purposes that are often very far from historical and cultural interests. An example is the revolutionary use of the photography by Giacomo Boni, who successfully experimented the approach of the aerial photography for archaeological sites, even at the end of the 19th century. The use of GIS (Geographic Information System) also has given a new impetus to topographical studies and has greatly simplified the management and analysis of spatial data, making it an almost indispensable tool for these areas of research.

Nevertheless, the obstacles to approaching three-dimensional surveying are many and varied. These include (i) a misuse of three-dimensional survey methodology for the purposes of an archaeological study traditionally based on two-dimensional documentation and (ii) a lack of ability to autonomously use the methodologies without relying on third parties.

As concerns the first issue, perhaps the worst mistake made by those who have believed in such practices from the inception, among which myself, is what I would call 'the pretension of objectivity'. There are a lot of papers on 3D experiments in archaeology that praise the objectivity of restitution as the great revolution in field surveys. Unlike happens with drawing, new survey methods are not affected by interpretations, the data is total and real, nothing is lost in the documentation. Suddenly the 3D restitution was considered superior while the 2D drawing was outdated, obsolete and even misleading! Many researchers forgotten what drawing meant for the archaeological documentation. In fact, since 2D information was always required from 3D model, the most disparate software was interrogated to "slice" millions and millions of points from the clouds generated by laser scanning and photogrammetry, with not always satisfactory results.

As concerns the second issue, we should consider that this new methodology (like so many others, sadly!) was not born for archaeology. It was first and foremost used and extensively tested in the industrial and engineering fields. Hence, for a long time only the engineers have been competent in the adoption of such tools. Although archaeology today is trying to recover its autonomy in this field, we are still far from a true 3D education of the discipline. This issue is of paramount importance because the archaeologist, if cannot fully understand the new ways of acquiring and restoring information, hardly can obtain a specific product for the purpose of his research.

1.1 The debate in the scientific community

The advance of new expedite three-dimensional acquisition methodologies, and specifically that of laser scanner and terrestrial and aerial photogrammetry, in the field of Cultural Heritage, has opened, also in archaeology, new scenarios and capabilities for survey.

An accurate reconstruction of the 3D is to be considered as a 'database' that preserves the passages and the methodology used by the ancient architect and allows to highlight how much of the original structure remains and the changes occurred over time.

The digital model elaborated after the survey, collects the data necessary to obtain information about the design and the choices (aesthetic and functional) made by the ancient architect[5].

In the last 20 years there has been a lot of discussions about equipment, grade of accuracy, acquisition, production times, costs and better software; little has been, nonetheless, done to systematically introduce a 3D research methodology within the archaeologist's routine[6]. 3D is often understated with regards to its metric and analytical content, whilst it is praised for its ability to a realistic representation of reality. This has favoured its use

---

[4] The experiment was carried out in building 89 (v. Berggren et al. 2015; Forte et al. 2015)

[5] Adembri et al 2016
[6] El-Hakim et al. 2004; Guidi et al. 2003; Campana, Remondino 2008; Novaković et al. 2017

in the dissemination and enjoyment of cultural heritage by diminishing the potential for research.

The approach to three-dimensional thinking in archaeology is not that recent as one could imagine. Already in 1989 Paul Reilly, in the article "Data visualization in archaeology"[7], spoke about the scientific importance of 3D reconstruction underlying the lack of an adequate theoretical background. In fact, already then (the first three-dimensional reproduction took place around 1985) the focus was on the actors carrying out such exercise, as the archaeologist that could not do other than leave the path clear to the graphic/modeler. Another current issue dealt with by Paul Reilly was the sheer amount of data to deal with in archaeology.

Railly asserts: *"[modelling] allows the researcher to demonstrate in strong visual terms how the interpretation relates directly to the collected data. [. . .] it stimulates the researcher to look for further information. This may involve the application of extra analytical experiments on the existing data, or it may require the formulation of a completely new research design to answer the outstanding questions."*[8]

Despite the scientific debate on the subject that has lasted through time and to which a number of privilege communication channels have been dedicated such as the ISPRS (International Society for Photogrammetry and Remote Sensing), the ICOMOS (International Council on Monuments and Sites), the CIPA (ICOMOS/ISPRS Committee for Documentation of Cultural Heritage) or the CAA (Computer Applications and Quantitative Methods in Archaeology, that since 70 dedicates annual conferences to the subject of technological innovation applied to archaeology); even today persists that which could be defined as a communication problem between the traditional and computational archaeology.

The computational archaeologists test the limits of the instruments available, demonstrating the capacity of software and showing how these can be used to register, analyse and present archaeological sites and artefacts, but continues to fail a real integration with what is the traditional diagnostics of archaeological documentation.

To be accepted by an ample community, a methodology must be comprehensive and able to be assessed. Often, however, publications relating to digital technology omit the process that led to their results, creating a closed system unable to offer anything for future research[9].

1.2 Innovative technologies

The survey for Cultural Heritage, even traditional, is often considered a sort of challenge for the professional, given the peculiarity (frequently the uniqueness) of the object surveyed, that leads always, even the most experienced operators, to adopt unconventional methods of acquisition.

If, often, beyond the subject, such difficulty is due to the lack of suitable tools for acquisitions, far more frequent the difficulty lays in the operational environment. Often in archaeology 'multi-scale' surveys are required, where an object is acquired in great detail with reference to the surrounding context. This requires, both different methodologies and tools for survey, and to operate with a homogeneity able to connect two results so different from each other[10].

The accuracy of a graphic restitution in the field of archaeology may vary significantly depending on the object of the survey and its purpose. The manufactured that require, due to their own characteristics, a precise millimetric or sub-millimetric, are not few.

Even if the total station is an instrument frequently used in contemporaneous archaeological excavations, some limitations reduce its use, especially regarding third dimension. The main limit is represented by the amount of time required to acquire the data due to the manual process of capturing the information. The use of reference values, or, alternatively, the manual positioning of a reflecting prism on each point subject to registration, are time-consuming operations. On the other hand, the precision in the execution of these survey operations is strongly dependent on the operator. That "human factor" influences the high precision level of the instrument. Moreover, an important aspect is that the analysis obtained with the total station does not return information on colours or materials that form part of the surveyed structure.

During the last decades a myriad of techniques, for these reasons, have been introduced in the field of archaeology to compensate these data losses[11]. These instruments allow one to have great versatility and practical use even in complex environmental conditions, be it in close proximity to the object that must be acquired (Close Range) be it for the structures (e.g., buildings or entire settlement) that require a wider range of action.

Understanding these innovative instruments becomes essential for the operators of cultural heritage, it is not necessary for the participation of the archaeologists, but to lead the right enquires and ease communications with surveyor. In fact, it is very important to have clarified the scope of the survey to be able to put in place the most adequate method to obtain the right resolution and level of accuracy.

Modern technologies of analysis, however, acquire too much data, which needs, during the elaboration phase, some filters, decimations and, therefore, reductions, in

[7] Reilly 1989
[8] Reilly 1989 p.577
[9] Ducke 2012

[10] Bitelli 2002
[11] Eisenbeiss et al., 2005; Tsiafaki, Michailidou 2015

order to allow a manageable reading and interpretation. These delicate passages carried out in the lab are also followed by the archaeologist or the conservation expert architect (depending on the research) to avoid the risk of losing too much information or erring in the interpretation of the data.

In field of archaeological research, the constant updating and development of technology and tools for three-dimensional survey, allows for a potentially development of 3D documentation project for stratigraphic excavation. This would allow a completely objective registration of data, providing a truthful and real representation of the terrain, for example, and structure and not only a simple synthetic model of the same.

The key aspects linked to the development of a 3D documentation of archaeological excavation and architectural structures can be summarized in:

1. truthful reconstruction of the excavation/structure/monument in their three dimensions;
2. deleting of subjectivisms in the planimetric representation of the stratigraphic deposit;
3. speed of acquisition (in particular if in use of a laser scanner);
4. measurement of the excavation/structure/monument in its three dimensions (X, Y, Z);
5. ability to crosscheck 3D information with 2D information;
6. ability to easily georeferenced the survey;
7. ease of reading the three-dimensional data;
8. completeness of the survey.

Nowadays the most used three-dimensional survey techniques in cultural heritage are the image-based (aerial and terrestrial photogrammetry) and the range-based (laser scanner) (Figure 2).

1.2.1 Photogrammetry

Photogrammetry is the science to obtain reliable metric information on physical objects through photography. Such methodology developed in the 20th century predominantly in topography, cartography and architecture, to develop maps or drawing complex architectural buildings facades.

Photogrammetry may be monoscopic or stereoscopic. The former considers a single resuming point and allows a bi-dimensional recovery of the data, whilst the latter, that employs the same principle as the human eye, has two resuming points obtaining the so called 'pair', allowing for three-dimensional recovery. Both techniques originally required the use of a metric or semi-metric camera. These cameras guarantee that the lens has no distortions; the optic axis is perpendicular to the film plane and that it is at a known distance from the centre of the frame. For the stereoscopic double-cameras are employed, placed on a tripod to which an arm is added at which ends the cameras are located, that guaranties the position at equal length of each other. The stereometric pair is than read through special stereoscopes.

1.2.2 Image-based survey

Image-based technique, that is the technique that produces the survey based on photographic images, is widely used in archaeology for 3D acquisition of structures and objects. This methodology is identified as 'close-range photogrammetry' when the object is situated at a distance below 300 m from the camera (this is also true for aerial shooting by drone). Originally linked to analytical photogrammetry, it has spung off, thanks to the acquisition of automatic techniques developed in the field of Computer Vision, where the projective geometry of vision is analysed and reinterpret through computers.

For example, whilst in a usual photogrammetric work an operator would carefully select a series of control points

Surveying

- Total Station
- GNSS

Range - based
(active sensors)

- Laser scanner (Triangulation scanner; Time of Flight and Phase shift)

Image - based
(passive sensors)

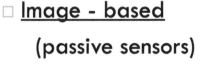

- Cameras and sensors (terrestrial and aerial) for SfM application

Figure 2. Pattern of techniques and instruments for 3D survey.

through a small number of images to create good matches, Computer Vision can extract thousands of such points from a big number of images, establishing automatically the matches among them.

This technique is used, beyond architectural survey, and in general, cultural heritage, also in the description of natural events such as land movements, rockfalls, or at industrial level in the study of deformations derived from sampling by stress.

The procedure is based on a series of images taken without a particular shooting order and ensuring an overlap of about 70% between the various shots and maintaining unchanged, throughout the shooting, the setting of the camera (focal exposure parameters, shutter speed, ISO). There is no quantitative limit in the photo shooting, but it must be borne in mind that a high level of images slows down significantly the calculation process and can damage the hardware if it is not adequate. That will depend on the purpose of the survey and the conditions linked to the shooting environment, rather than the object or the tools employed. In fact, even with a modest sample of images one can obtain detailed modelling. With regards to archaeological excavations, given that this is a unique and destructive operation, it is recommended to acquire a high number of shots. The selection of good images can be subsequently done, before continuing the process with the software. It is paramount to remember that an object will only be represented in three dimensions if present in at least three images (Figure 3).

Nowadays, there are multiple software in the field of digital photogrammetry. Commercial software allows control of all the phases of processing and for the management of different post-production parameters. However, they are limited in that they rely on the hardware on which they are installed. Little RAM or limited HD can be the cause of interruption of processes or of extreme slowdown of the same, especially if large photographic sets were required. On the other hand, a web-based processing platform allows you not to burden your pc but limits the control of the execution procedures.

During processing, the Structure from Motion (SfM) algorithms allow you to reconstruct the shape of objects through the automatic collimation of points from the set of photos acquired. Key points are extracted from the single photos, taking the photographic parameters and crossing the recognizable points (pixels) on several photos and, in this way, the coordinates are identified in the location of the points themselves. The software generates a point cloud (sparse cloud) characterized by 6 values that define the position in location and colour[12].

The greater the homologous points recognized in the feature matching phase, the denser the point clouds generated.

On the basis of this it is possible to generate a mesh model or to recreate the surfaces of the detected object, and apply the texture on it which, clearly, is processed on the basis of the shots taken. The 3D model obtained in this way is scaled according to coordinates of known topographic points, recognized on the photos themselves and entered manually, or automatically with GPS data, if you use photographic equipment with this integrated tool, thanks to the information contained in the EXIF data of the individual photos. In this way 3D is measurable and any extracted graphic information (ortho-photos, sections, plans, etc.) is geometrically correct.

To ensure metric correctness and check for errors, you must interpret each phase of the survey and make sure the equipment is suitable for use. The difference between a 3D model and a 3D 'survey' lies in this.

To determine the resolution of a digital image, and consequently the scale with which it is possible to make a photogrammetric survey, it is essential to know the size of the camera sensor (of its pixels) and the distance of acquisition of the images from the object. The *Ground Sample Distance* (GSD) represents the distance between the centre of two consecutive pixels expressed in territorial units. In other words, it expresses the "quantity of reality" contained in a pixel.

This relationship between the real unit of measurement (the meter) and the digital one of the images (the pixel) is, therefore, used to ensure that a photogrammetric survey is represented on a precise scale. The smaller the GSD, the more detailed the information contained in the relative pixel will be[13].

It is clear that the GSD is subject to variations due to the acquisition distance, the characteristics of the camera sensor and the optics used. It is therefore necessary to know all this data to determine it and then program a photogrammetric survey at a certain scale.

To know the size of the single pixel of a photographic sensor, simply search for the characteristics of the camera you are using[14], the focal distance, however, depends on the lenses you choose to use. What can vary more easily is the shooting distance of the object to be acquired. Referring to the following proportion:

$$d : D = f : H$$

where the "d" defines the pixel size, the "D" refers to the acquired object size, or the GSD, the "f" indicates the focal distance and the "H" values the distance of the shooting point from the object, we will be able to obtain, with a

---

[12] Remondino *et al.* 2014

[13] For example, if an ortho-photo has a GSD of 0.20 m/pix (20 cm real in each pixel) while another has a GSD of 0.02 m/pix (2 cm real in each pixel), we can say that the second is far more detailed than the first.
[14] This data is easily obtainable from dedicated websites (e.g. https://www.dpreview.com)

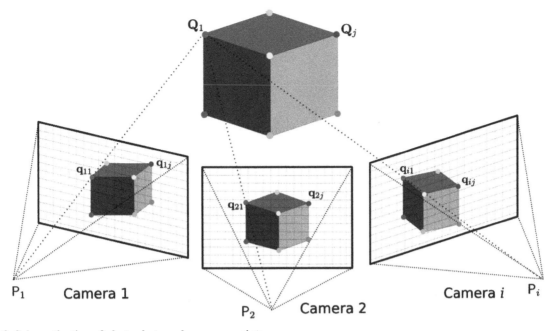

Figure 3. Schematization of photo shots and recovery points.

simple calculation, the necessary data. So, the GSD can be obtained this way:

GSD = H *d/f*

But, with a simple change of the factors, you can get the value of the distance you need to keep to get a specific GSD (Figure 4).

The aerial photogrammetric survey provides that the sensors and digital cameras, or the indispensable tools for acquiring images for this type of topographic work, are mounted on aerial platforms of different types (airplanes, balloons, kites, helicopters, etc.), or satellite (Ikonos, World-View, Spot, Quickbird, etc.) (Figure 5).

High altitude aerial photogrammetry is widely used for the production of precision cartographic and topographical data, such as:

- production and updating of topographic maps (national maps 1:100,000, 1:50,000 or 1:25,000);
- production and updating of numerical cartography into GIS system;
- production of Digital Terrain Models (DTM);
- orthophotos;
- production of thematic maps (geological, hydrological, forestry. . .) in scale 1: 25.000 or 1: 10.000;
- large scale map production for urban and regional planning (regional techniques 1: 10,000, 1: 5,000 or for civil engineering works 1: 2,000, 1,000, 500);
- cadastral maps and environmental surveys.

Increasingly, however, drones are used in the archaeological and architectural fields as they allow to acquire nadiral or oblique images and to obtain surveys of precision comparable to those obtained by laser scanners but at lower costs[15].

Micro-UAVs (Unmanned Aerial Vehicle) have recently been developed and with reduced costs allow great versatility of use. The survey from mini and micro-UAV guarantees the accurate restitution of surfaces and volumes, and therefore the construction of measurable three-dimensional replicas of high precision. Although, in fact, they generally do not mount sensors with very high resolution, their dimensions allow easy manoeuvrability at

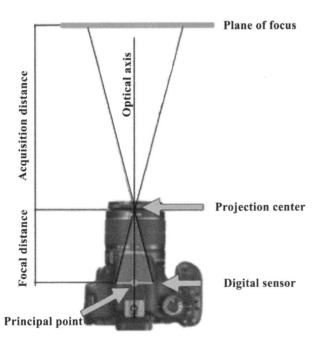

Figure 4. Graphic representation of the camera elements that contribute to the GSD calculation.

---
[15] Remondino et al. 2011

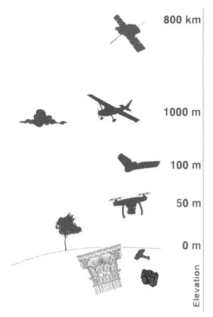

800 km

1000 m

100 m

50 m

0 m

Elevation

Figure 5. support scheme for digital photogrammetry according to the acquisition elevation.

The digital photogrammetric shooting technique is defined as terrestrial which is used at ground level. The cameras do not necessarily require specific support (as in the past), but can be hand-held, mounted on tripods or other specially designed supports.

This method is used with a common photographic camera, the specifications of which will change according to the type of intervention and the detail to be obtained (Figure 6). This feature makes this method potentially 'low cost' compared to the aerial technique.

The terrestrial digital photogrammetry technique, by its nature, allows great versatility of use and freedom of movement. It is widely used for survey for engineering and architectural applications, such as:

- precision measurements for industrial structures;
- survey for deformation and damages control, as well as to carry out surveys of objects that are not easily accessible or accessible for a limited time;
- reconstruction of road accidents;
- survey of living organisms;
- documentation and survey of cultural heritage.

In the archaeological field the terrestrial digital photogrammetry technique is highly appreciated and used because it allows to operate in complex environmental situations, allowing, however, rapid acquisition and high detail.

very low altitudes thus allowing very close acquisitions and, consequently, great detail.

By using these aerial vehicles in archaeology, it is possible to perform multi-temporal investigations, programming flights with same parameters at different times of the excavation campaign, and obtain photogrammetric surveys of low altitude archaeological sites, 3D models and ortho-photos.

It is possible to carry out an analysis of the areas built for the reading of the ancient road system and the relationships between it and the buildings, for a better understanding of the evolution dynamics of the urban fabric and paleo-morphologies, as well as planning inspections and detailed photographic surveys of architectural structures (aqueducts, monuments, fortifications, etc.).

The possibility of equipping UAVs with sensors other than RGB (chosen according to the purpose of the research) such as NIR (Near Infrared), multi- or hyper-spectral and thermal, very useful for identifying anomalies on the ground and therefore functional, in the archaeological field, to support recognition.

These tools allow also inspections of architectural structures in inaccessible or small-sized interiors thanks to the use of "micro-drones" and in the field work, they provide support for immediate documentation of the various stratigraphic excavation phases in its entirety and for a 3D and 2D graphic mapping and restitution which allows the analysis of the different stratigraphic phases and their visualization in their original position even long time after the excavation[16].

The aim of the terrestrial photogrammetric survey is to provide precise data on shape, size and position of a specific structural remain or monument, at a given moment and to evaluate its actual conditions and architectural aspects.

In recent years, this method has been widely used for the documentation of the archaeological excavation in progress, attempting to outline a specific workflow for this type of field surveys[17].

Thanks to the combination with metric and topographical reference systems, surveys with sub-centimetric accuracy are obtained. The coordinate system that will be chosen depends mainly on the size of an object to be acquired. GPS systems and global coordinate systems are practical to use only for huge objects and where high-level hardware equipment is available. A local coordinate system is used frequently to surveyed architectural elements or restricted areas.

---

[16] An important issue is the regulation of the use of such instruments. The rule in question is constantly evolving. The ENAC (National Civil

Aviation Authority) indications on this subject have been subject to numerous changes in recent years, as it has been faced with an increase in purchases of this equipment and applications even in situations considered to be at risk. It is therefore now necessary to hold a specific license to fly such aircraft. Before carrying out a job involving the use of APR, it is necessary to make sure that you have all the characteristics in compliance with the regulations and request permission to fly from ENAC. All information and forms can be found on their website: https://www.enac.gov.it/sicurezza-aerea/droni (last access May 2022)
[17] Lercari *et al.* 2017; Fiorini 2013

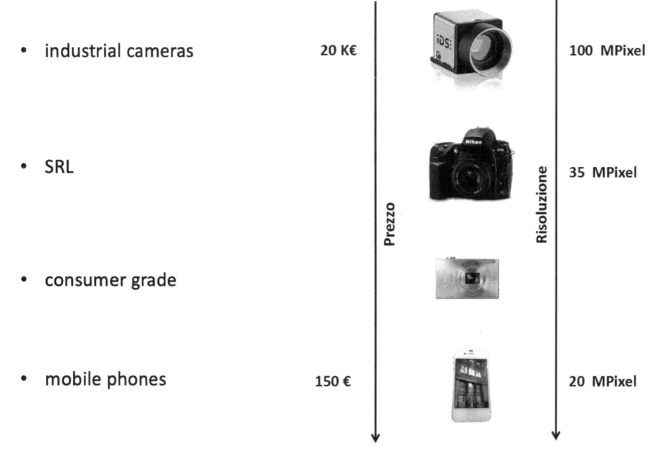

- industrial cameras   20 K€   100 MPixel

- SRL   35 MPixel

- consumer grade

- mobile phones   150 €   20 MPixel

Figure 6. Types of cameras for photogrammetry.

1.2.3 Laser scanner

3D scanners are tools capable of acquiring point clouds automatically and at high speed thanks to the projection of a light beam or pattern on the object and analysis of the return signal.

The possibility of obtaining a huge number of information measured and positioned in space (even global, thanks to the presence of GPS integrated in the machines), has encouraged the use of such equipment in numerous fields, from engineering to medicine, to geology, architecture and also cultural heritage.

The use of laser scanners in archaeological field, for example, allows obtaining accuracy of acquisitions close to the millimetre within a radius of 10 meters, allowing to create a 3D system in which to gradually insert the found stratigraphic units[18].

Laser scanners are divided into:

- *Triangulation scanners*, in which the emitter and receiver are separated. The distance between them is known and the measurements are calculated with the

triangulation system. The precision of the survey is also sub-millimetre.
- *Direct scanners*, in which the position of the emitter and the signal receiver coincide, and the precision in the measurement is in the order of millimetres, if the scanned object is in the proximity, or centimetres if this it is more distant.

Each laser scanner differs for specific parameters related to the type of laser, the operating system and the internal electronics[19]. These characteristics determine their choice according to the needs related to the single survey campaign (Figure 7).

At the end of the acquisition operations there is a point cloud for each shooting position, at very high density, that allows you to view in great detail the object detected. Although it is a set of points, and not a compact surface, the result, especially if acquired with high resolution settings and at medium-close distance, is very clear, thanks to the incredible number of points acquired. These points, as mentioned above, can bring RGB data with them if the scanner has an integrated photographic camera, thus allowing an even more realistic result. Modern scanners have made the acquisition phase very intuitive as well as

---

[18] Peripimeno 2005

[19] Guidi 2014

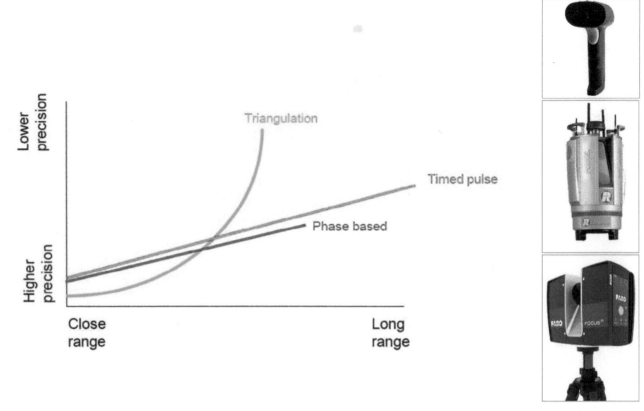

Figure 7. Distance / precision diagram of the different types of laser scanners.

expeditious; what, unfortunately, continues to be a rather long and laborious process is the post processing of the acquired data, the key element for the construction of a correct survey.

The processing takes place through special software, generally proprietary software, and which allows for the performance the operations that will allow you to move from the raw data to the structured information. It may be necessary to clean the scans before recording, this is because, frequently, anomalies of points in the cloud are created due, for example, to reflective objects or moving objects being scanned.

The alignment of the individual scans can take place both through references arranged ad hoc (flat or spherical targets) in the shooting environment, and through natural references (planes, angles, surfaces . . .), it is therefore good practice not to go overboard with the "cleaning" of extraneous things to the object of the survey to ensure greater overlapping elements and alignment of the scans[20].

---

[20] The alignment of the scans can take several steps; as mentioned, artificial targets, that are automatically recognized by the software, can facilitate their placement. The recognition of homologous points between the shots can also be done manually, once a certain number of common points have been entered, the software will carry out the matching. The latest laser scanning systems allow the alignment of individual scans (point clouds) in real time, in field, thanks to special software that recognize the scanner position and characteristics of the acquired surfaces. The processing takes place on special tablets or PCs.

Some latest generation systems allow the laser scanner to be used even on the move (on quads, cars, boats, helicopters . . .) thanks to the association of other sensors such as cameras, GPS and Inertial Measurement Units (IMU). The so-called MMS (Mobile Mapping System) exploits the potential of the movement and speed of the platform on which the scanner is mounted, to acquire data faster. By synchronizing the data with the GPS positioning system and the inertial system, centimetre accuracy is achieved.

Even the latest total stations can be programmed to work in "scanner" mode but the performances, in terms of acquisition speed and, therefore, of detectable dot density and resolution, are lower than those of a laser scanner.

In total stations, the measurement of distance is carried out by making repeated measurements, which allow to obtain high accuracy and eliminate same principal errors. Laser scanners, on the other hand, use systems for signal deflection that allow very small rotations and use simplified algorithms for processing the return signal. This results in less accuracy than topographic distance meters. The standard deviation for measuring the distances of the TOF (Time of Flight) scanners is always a few millimetres greater than the total stations.

1.3 Data management

For an archaeological "object" to be subject to an adequate conservation strategy, an integrated representation of various types of relevant information is required. For this reason, the digital management of the information of the archaeological heritage is still not straightforward.

In the mid-1990s, various scientific organizations and scientific committees started defining standards for the digital preservation. These included standards for descriptive, technical, conservation and structural metadata.

Early on, digital preservation was conceived as a series of discrete and very specific technical activities, aimed at obtaining reliable and usable digital objects. However, more recently, conservation has become a subset of 'digital curation' activities aimed at managing digital objects throughout their entire life cycle, from creation and acquisition, to conservation, access and reuse. The terminology is far from being well-established as this area of research continues to develop and grow[21].

1.3.1 Metadata

Scientific data cannot be correctly interpreted and reused without knowing how it was created and in what circumstances.

Metadata is used to evaluate:

- meaning (visualization, experimental setting, instrument settings);
- relevance (the things represented, their status, their conditions);
- quality (calibration, tolerances, errors);
- possibility of improvement and adaptation.

For the 3D digitalization all these aspects are relevant because of the range of technologies, tools and methodologies available for capturing and processing data and the diversity of motivations and reasons behind any 3D digital replica.

Metadata can store information on the life cycle of a 3D object from its generation to storage and subsequent uses. Metadata allows practitioners in this field to keep track of the instrument settings (calibration, tolerances and errors), of the physical object (general state and conditions) and the possibilities to improve or adapt the model.

It is crucial that standards on content of metadata are sufficiently flexible and enable the rapid acquisition and processing of digital collections – especially if the material is stored on unstable media. Minimum descriptive metadata such as title, creator, donor, date and a unique identifier (generated by the system), will ensure that the material can be recovered for further processing in the future.

1.3.2 Digital Curation

'Digital curation' is about maintaining, preserving and adding value to digital research data over their life cycle (Figure 8). Active management of research data can maximize its long-term value and reduce the risk of digital obsolescence. This is because the data, when properly maintained in specific and reliable digital repositories, can be shared among the wider research community.

Digital curation helps decrease the efforts required to creating research data. It also increases the long-term value of existing data by making it available for further research (i.e., 'data reuse'). Digital curation and data retention, however, are ongoing processes. Conservation activities must be planned prior to their implementation, to ensure the long-term protection of the authority of the digital material. Such activities include validation, assignment of retention metadata, assignment of information, and assurance of acceptable data structures or file formats.

The London Charter for the Computer-based Visualization of Cultural Heritage[22] (hereafter the London Charter) was conceived, in 2006, as a means of ensuring the methodological rigor of computer-based visualization – especially when researching and communicating cultural heritage.

The London Charter is the most advanced international document in this field. Its various updates reveal the need to a document including best practices on how to plan new cultural heritage research activities, it also reflects the demand for new recommendations and orientations tailored to the specific needs of the different researches' fields and communities of experts. For this reason, the objectives set out in the London Charter aim to provide a solid foundation on which communities of experience can build detailed implementation guidelines of its principles.

We should be mindful of the wide scope of cultural heritage, it includes monumental, ethnographic, documentary, industrial, artistic, archaeological and oral heritage. We cannot stress enough how important it is ensuring that digital visualization methods are applied with academic rigor. The research results based on digital visualization should always make it clear to the users what the state of art is by distinguishing between evidence and hypothesis and the level of confidence in these.

The London Charter aims to strengthen the rigor of the methods and the results of digital visualization and how these are used and evaluated in different cultural contexts. The ultimate objective is to ensure the recognition of the methods and the results. The London Charter defines principles for the use of digital visualization methods in relation to:

---

[21] Kott 2012

[22] http://www.londoncharter.org

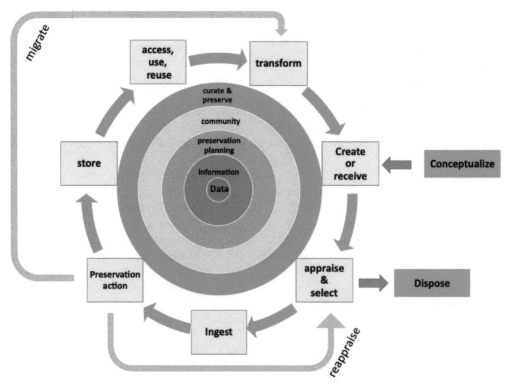

Figure 8. The life-cycle of digital data. (Adapted from the model by Sarah Higgins)

1. intellectual integrity;
2. reliability;
3. documentation;
4. sustainability;
5. accessibility[23].

Just one year after the London Charter, the Ename Charter (ICOMOS – International Council on Monuments and Sites) reiterated the need that any graphic reconstructions must be based on evidence collected by using commonly accepted scientific and research methods. This includes the analysis of written texts, oral and iconographic sources and photographic documentation. All sources used for alternative reconstructions must be provided so as to allow comparison[24].

The 2008 Seville Charter[25] sponsored by the Spanish Society of Virtual Archaeology (SEAV), reaffirmed the principles of the London Charter by reiterating the importance of transparency and scientific reliability of the

archaeological data in virtual reconstructions. The Seville Charter proposed a definition of 'virtual archaeology' and numerous other aspects related to it – this received consensus by the scientific community.

Virtual archaeology is defined as "the scientific discipline that seeks to research and develop ways of using computer-based visualization for the comprehensive management of archaeological heritage"[26].

Generation of new knowledge is possible only if the digital structures and data adhere to certain principles that guarantee reliability. In 2016 was published the guidelines defined by the FAIR principles: the data must be Findable (they must be retrievable), Accessible (once found, the data must be accessible, permissions and authentications included), Interoperable (the data must be able to be integrated with other data and interact with different workflows), Reusable (reuse of the data must be optimized, through the addition of a comprehensive description that allows replicability). Through the application of these principles, the data will be part of a dynamic global reuse process within larger knowledge networks.

1.3.3 Provenance and Paradata

In order to certify the reliability of the data it is essential to define a formal semantics for the minimum content that can simplify the reuse of the certifies information.

---

[23] Of particular interest in this research is the following principle:
Principle 4:
Documentation 'Sufficient information should be documented and disseminated to allow computer-based visualisation methods and outcomes to be understood and evaluated in relation to the contexts and purposes for which they are deployed.'
Principle 4.6: Documentation of Process ('Paradata')
Documentation of the evaluative, analytical, deductive, interpretative and creative decisions made in the course of computer-based visualisation should be disseminated in such a way that the relationship between research sources, implicit knowledge, explicit reasoning, and visualisation-based outcomes can be understood.
[24] www.international.icomos.org
[25] http://www.arqueologiavirtual.com

[26] http://www.vi-mm.eu/wp-content/uploads/2016/10/The-Seville-Principles.pdf

This process includes notice on the origin of the data in the metadata model, i.e. the process that determined the digitization of the physical object[27].

'Provenance' can be defined as the description of the technical processes involved in the creation of digital objects. It covers processes such as:

- chosen equipment and tool settings
- sources of light
- obstacles to digitization or sources of noise and/or light reflections
- software choices and settings
- techniques chosen for meshing, texture, decimation, simplification, alignment, etc.

Another aspect crucial to the correct definition of the digital data is the information that allow to understand and interpret the data; these are called 'paradata'.

In a nutshell, the paradata are descriptions, within a research project, of the evidence used to interpret an artefact. These include the reconstruction and a description of the methodological premises of the research. They define the context in which the model is created and manipulated also for further investigations or reconstructions (Human process).

Provenance and paradata information within the metadata are therefore essential to a correct reuse of any digital data and, perhaps even more decisively, for a three-dimensional model. They have been implemented as part of the metadata schemes for Cultural Heritage, since they help the user to verify the quality of the data and to avoid errors in the evaluation of the source. They also allow one to check the parameters and the methods chosen in the construction of the 3D object. For example, they allow, to establish what tool was used for acquisitions, how many scans were performed and what was the method and software used for alignment.

With reference to these issues in the field of cultural heritage, noteworthy is the 3D-ICONS project[28]. It is a pilot project funded under the ICT Policy Support Program, based on the projects: CARARE and 3DCOFORM[29]. The aim of 3D-ICONS was to provide Europeana[30], the famous digital library of European culture, with a large number of three-dimensional objects, videos and photos complete with freely searchable metadata. The

partnership was composed of 16 institutions with long experience in digitizing architecture, buildings and archaeological monuments in 3D. The project ended on 31 January 2015. During the project, 3D-ICONS developed a specific metadata scheme for recording the life cycle of a 3D datum, which includes aspects of provenance and paradata.

1.3.4 Repository

'Digital repository' can be used in a number of contexts with different meanings. In academia it generally refers to archives that researchers can use to share articles and documents. Digital repositories are used to manage digital resources. Some of these are in digital format from the very beginning, others were converted in digital format as originally the came from material previously archived analogically, e.g., photographs and documents.

Some repositories have been built around the somewhat heavy and rigid standards developed in the late 90s and early 2000s and with a focus on digital library collections. These were impossible to use for smaller organizations and presented significant challenges also for the large ones.

Over time a number of guidelines have been developed to help create tailor-made solutions for the different needs. The choice of the reference standards is then fundamental. The Open Archival Information Standard (OAIS)[31] providers a useful reference model. The purpose of the OAIS model is to establish metadata and packaging framework to ensure that what is deposited can then be recovered and used again in other circumstances.

There is a clear need for repositories that guarantee peer-review of published 3D models and, therefore, a clear recognition of their validity. Such tools are essential to respect the principle of data transparency.

1.3.5 On-line 3D visualization

The issue of on-line visualization of complex 3D graphic elaborations has long been the subject of debate and research. Currently, some recently developed solutions are used which, in large part, are satisfactory, although it doesn't cover all the needs.

A revolution in the matter took place in 2010, with the release of the WebGL standard[32], JavaScript graphics API designed specifically to integrate Web and 3D, this is to create solutions that would allow 3D content to be integrated into browsers like other multimedia layers (images, audio, video).

---

[27] D'Andrea 2013

[28] http://3dicons-project.eu

[29] The objective of the CARARE programme is the detailed description of the heritage, the events in which these assets have been involved on information on where digital resources can be reached online (http://www.carare.eu/). 3D-COFORM aims to introduce new tools for the creation of 3D representations of artworks, creating links also to other information and for use in different applications. (http://3dcoform.eu).

[30] Europeana provides free access to millions of digital resources provided by over 2000 European institutions. To facilitate harvesting Europeana has developed a metadata scheme (EDM) on which individual standards can be easily mapped (http://www.europeana.eu).

[31] Standard ISO 14721:2012.

[32] https://www.khronos.org/webgl/

Sketchfab[33] is a tool widely used for the diffusion of 3D models of any kind on the web and of which the branch of cultural heritage is also making great use.

Many important international museums are exploiting this platform to create low-cost virtual museum rooms to share objects from their collections.

3DHOP[34] (3D Heritage Online Presenter) is the product of a research group, the ISTI-CNR Visual Computing Lab, designed specifically for the Cultural Heritage sector, for advanced web sharing 3D content[35]. 3DHOP uses a multi-resolution coding, which allows you to efficiently manage high resolution 3D models used in applications for Cultural Heritage.

Born for research, it is a totally Open-source support, compatible with all browsers and operating systems. The user can configure the viewer, customizing it with specific tools (tools for measurements, to obtain sections in one of the three axes or, also, a directional light that allows to simulate the lighting of the real environment).

1.3.6 Management systems

Nowadays, three-dimensional digital models of architectural heritage are considered indispensable representations for the heterogeneous management of data.

However, the transition from two-dimensional drawings to 3D models is a complex process that is not limited to the creation of volumetric objects. Conservation professionals need not only to navigate documents but also to perform multi-criteria queries in a virtual 3D environment to make decisions aimed at interventions. A "simple" 3D geometric object is therefore not sufficient, as it lacks, for example, any information on its internal structure and on the mutual relationships between the various architectural elements (semantics). This conceptual organization is of great importance. If the 3D geometric model is enriched by reciprocal and hierarchical relationships, access to information can be more efficient.

The management process can be divided into three main phases: the conceptual modelling, the data structuring

and the data representation[36]. In addition to geometry, architectural heritage objects contain a large amount of heterogeneous data due to their physical and historical complexity. For this reason, they need a lot of different information besides 3D data[37]. In this context, the representations must structure the definition and relational characteristics. At the same time, it is essential to integrate different types of data with the geometric characteristics to access and structure the information.

The great digital revolution for archaeology reached its peak in the 90s of the last century, when GIS (Geographic Information System) became part of the assortment of software used for the geo-referencing of archaeological sites and for the cataloguing of findings through the use of relational databases[38]. In this way, the degree of precision reallocating excavations and discoveries became very high.

This system has also gradually adapted with the development of three-dimensional elaborations. Although, GIS, rather than 3D, is 4D, since it adds time to the three dimensions of space[39].

The realism with which information is made explicit in the software makes the latter a very valuable tool, first of all, for architectural purposes, for urban planning and for infrastructure projects. It is possible to view a large amount of information such as, for example, a large city in 3D, also thanks to data models such as CityGML[40], or a data standard that allows you to have different levels of detail (LOD) depending on the points of view.

The traditional excavation's GIS is modified by this new 3D approach. That which was an overlap of the different floor plans and some rare DTM (Digital Terrain Model), opens to the third dimension. With the three-dimensional visualization of the stratigraphic deposits, geo-referenced with spatial coordinates (X, Y, Z), it is possible to have a complete view of the excavation phases and the finds, eliminating any distortion due to interpretations or simplifications of the traditional design[41] (Figure 9).

The very recent work by Dell'Unto and Landeschi[42] is strictly focused on the application of 3D GIS technology to the archaeological context. The book, updated to several case studies, provides practical examples (e.g., using material from Pompeii, Çatalhöyük, as well as prehistoric and protohistoric sites in Southern Scandinavia) to solve specific problems (i.e., integration of traditional GIS and 3D modelling, application to different context such as excavations, landscapes and buildings).

---

[33] Sketchfab allows you to enter some annotations and metadata to the navigable model. The information specific to the monument can also be added directly to the model in the form of numbered interactive windows. The progressive numbering also allows to create a sort of explanatory path of the object to guide the user to its comprehension. However, the organization of the metadata is not well structured. It allows, in fact, the free compilation of some information that can be related to the object itself (history, type, general description), or to the provenance (such as the type of instrumentation used for the acquisition), leaving, however, the choice to fill the fields or not. The templates are always related to the user profile that uploaded them and that must be, necessarily, provided and authenticated. The data relative to the type of file of the inserted model (resolution, size, extension), are automatically recognized and inserted in a specific section.
https://sketchfab.com/
[34] http://vcg.isti.cnr.it/3dhop/index.php
[35] Potenziani *et al.* 2015

[36] Saygi *et al.* 2013
[37] De Luca *et al.*, 2011
[38] Licheri 2016
[39] Forte 2014
[40] https://www.ogc.org/standards/citygml
[41] Peripimeno 2005
[42] Dell'Unto, Landeschi 2022

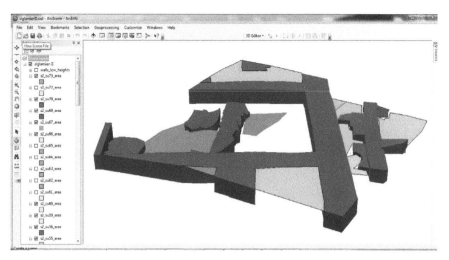

Figure 9. Example of 3D GIS from Seglamien excavation by University of Naples L'Orientale (Courtesy of Marco Barbarino).

Recently, a tool for reconstructive data management in archaeology has been developed. It is the Extended Matrix, a tool based on stratigraphic data as chronological and spatial data, in order to manage archaeological reconstructive information for both research and dissemination purposes[43].

The reconstruction is part of research and fundamental step for archaeological interpretation and subsequent analysis. Therefore, a reliable and scientifically valid reconstruction is indispensable. The Extended Matrix approach stems from the need to establish a standardised criterion for reconstruction in archaeology. It is based on a stratigraphic concept, applied to a specific 3D visualisation of the different structure's chronological phases.

By means of proxy models and colour-coded scales, the tool aims to facilitate the collaborative work of specialists from different disciplines. Using a graph database, the Extended Matrix generates a reconstructive record that includes the temporal relationships between elements. The EM was developed inspired by the classical Harris Matrix by adding the concept of virtual stratigraphic units.

Probably this type of approach, that is extremely familiar to archaeologists, finds its natural evolution in Building Information Modelling.

1.3.7 Building Information Modelling

The acronym BIM (Building Information Modelling) defines a new methodological process of design architectural data which is not simply a new modelling software. While it may seem obvious, preliminary definition issues are important here, as BIM has been interpreted variously by its different users. Among the numerous definitions of BIM, the one given by the NBIMS (National BIM Standard) is: "*A BIM is a digital*

representation of physical and functional characteristics of a facility. As such it serves as a shared knowledge resource for information about a facility forming a reliable basis for decisions during its lifecycle from inception onward." [44]

BIM is defined as a digital representation of the construction process to facilitate the exchange and interoperability of information in digital format. A complete set of design documents stored in an integrated database and information about the entire building are used in BIM. This information is totally parametric and interconnected.

Whatever the explanation we support, BIM cannot replace a designer or architect, nor is a standard protocol to be agreed. BIM is rather a philosophy or a framework process for collecting and managing different 3D datasets.

BIM has been implemented in modern civil engineering and architecture, in order to integrate the needs of designers with the world of companies and construction industries.

Therefore, it has little to do with the tangible archaeological heritage. However, thanks to its characteristics, BIM can easily connect various pieces of information relating to architectural and archaeological data. The archaeological heritage like a modern building, has a uniform approach that can combine in a single processing model different category of data, such as the description of individual architectural elements, the state of conservation, information on the spatial organization of the building, the use or reuse of spaces and objects, the classification of objects, etc.

The main challenge of BIM is to manage and share different datasets related to a building, during its complete life cycle, including geographic and alphanumeric data. Simplifying, BIM can be considered as an evolution of GIS, in that it is a software capable of managing spatial data, but in a 3D environment.

---

[43] Demetrescu 2018

[44] https://www.nationalbimstandard.org/about

The most appreciated feature of BIM system is the ability to freely share 3D data, providing several experts access to the same model or part of it. Thanks to BIM, each user can access, consult, assemble and modify any part of the model by actively participating in the same project. In this sense, it pushes various actors to collaborate, without obliging them to acquire a new language or sacrifice their attitudes or their professional background, and without risking the loss of information in the various format passages.

It is possible to integrate, in a common model, data from topographical reliefs, laser scans or photogrammetric 3D campaigns, as well as traditional architectural data, virtual models and all hypotheses and reconstructions. The co-presence of multiple models that connect with each other requires a good level of interoperability (physical and semantic) between the different approaches to allow different users and experts to work and cooperate, or simply to view a specific model or specific parts of it.

The strength of this system lies mostly in the Industry Foundation Classes (IFC) format, which is becoming the standard format for data exchange. It is an open-source format, not controlled by any software manufacturer, developed by the International Alliance for Interoperability (IAI) in order to convert into a standard that facilitates interoperability between programs in the construction and building sectors. Indeed, they allow to represent an object, its properties and its relationships with the other objects that make up an artefact. It is a stable format, in the version known as IFC2.X (where X stands for eXtensible) and which has an international character, since in accordance with ISO / PAS 16739. IFC guarantees a reduced loss of information in the exchange process between the various applications and actors.

Many studies have highlighted BIM maturity levels that define the technological progress achieved based on the degree of collaboration and information sharing between the different parties involved in a project. The maturity model[45] is the schema representing the evolutionary plan that the United Kingdom has established for the management of the building process through BIM methodology. It starts from level 0, where there is no collaboration (CAD phase), and goes up to the last level characterised by the use of cloud platforms and BIM models that guarantee a perfect integration of information (iBIM – interoperable data for BIM).

As concerns the study, documentation and valorisation of cultural heritage, the potential of BIM and GIS still presents strong criticalities, which grow even more in the field of archaeological evidence. Since these systems are not born for such purposes, they need a structuring of processes that can simultaneously manage the three-dimensional representation and the informative knowledge also in the geographic dimension. To fill these

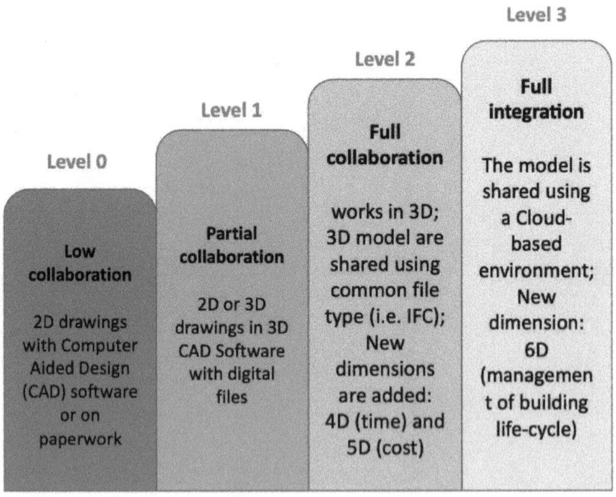

Figure 10. Schema of BIM maturity levels.

gaps, the latest research is experimenting with operational workflows that aim at interoperability between the two systems[46], by exploiting the three-dimensional modelling potential of BIM and the possibility of carrying out spatial analysis of GIS. This approach allows building multi-scalar and multidisciplinary information systems and then structure a unique and interoperable archive. On the other hand, there are still few works in literature that deal with the subject from the point of view of cultural heritage and less for archaeology[47]. In this domain, the exchange of data between the two systems needs to know the complex system of semantic relations that connect the concepts and, therefore, the elements of the built[48], often not uniquely definable.

---

[45] Bew, Richards 2008.

[46] Clemen 2022; Song et al. 2017; Ohori et al. 2017
[47] Matrone et al. 2019
[48] Schilling, Clemen 2022

2

Field Documentation

"Excavation and its documentation conform the analytical step of archaeological research" [1].

The purpose of excavation is to retrieve data and information, which the archaeologist scrupulously records in different ways: excavation diaries, cards, photos, sketches and precision topographic surveys obtained with different equipment. Any information not recorded in this way is lost.

Annotating excavation diaries has evolved over time, moving from a sort of travel story that exclusively emphasized the discoveries to a systematic (and as aseptic as possible) recording of facts and work responsibilities[2]. Similarly, the graphic documentation reduces any risk of loss of information or subjective interpretations.

The basic methods for documenting archaeological excavations have not changed much over the centuries. These techniques, familiar to anyone who has studied archaeology, are based on the use of a pencil, paper and meter to record as much as possible information about an excavation. These methods are direct surveying and therefore require the object to be accessible. Generally, the results are two-dimensional drawings; on which even the most experienced archaeologist will provide a general representation of the acquired area and not an objective recording of reality.

Whether it is a triangulation or cross section method, these surveying techniques accumulate deformations, even if perfectly set, due to the "flexibility" of the instruments and difficulties in their positioning (losing verticality of the meter, accumulating deformations and selections, despite being generally accepted.)[3].

These errors are strongly affected by scale and degree of simplification. They are generally considered acceptable due to the complexity of the objects in Cultural Heritage characterized by irregular geometry, often due to the action of time. Due to this, archaeological sites have offered food for thought for the execution and integration of geomatic techniques. The aim of the studies and activities of cultural heritage operators is to find, preserve and communicate these pieces of information.[4]

2.1 3D survey at excavation stage

Unlike traditional surveying techniques, the use of a 3D survey methodology on site, especially with photogrammetric technique, clashes with some environmental problems and requires, for this reason, an accurate design.

For example, lighting often becomes a problem given that archaeological sites are generally open and rather large spaces. In fact, while in a laboratory it is possible to modify the light source as required, on site the only lighting available is direct sunlight, which is variable in nature.

A lot of sunshine can generate strong light/shadow contrasts that are difficult to attenuate in the survey process, which affects the reading of parts of object. Also sudden changes in the light conditions during the survey can affect the results. With regards to photography, commonly used in traditional excavation documentation, the best conditions for 3D relief (especially for photogrammetric) are cloudy days, as they allow for uniform light on all surfaces.

Therefore, in large areas, it is extremely important to plan the survey in order to make sure that some parts are not left out; a distraction would result in a gap in the final processing and an irreversible loss of information, since excavation clearly is a destructive action.

Structure from Motion (SfM) technology, as mentioned above, works by analysing a series of photos with a high degree of overlap (taken from a variety of consistent angles) and finding among them homologous points that will be mutated into clouds of 3D points. This versatile technique is now widely used to document archaeological features and on-site materials, also due how realistic the final model is. This model is generated from photographs combined into a single photographic texture perfectly draped over the geometry. To achieve greater accuracy, the model can be scaled and oriented using topographic information acquired either simultaneously or at another time. Control points are positioned in the scene and measured using a total station or GPS. If GPS is used, differential GPS (dGPS) or Real-time Kinematic (RTK) will be required, since standard devices do not yet offer the accuracy needed to produce useful models.

Reference targets in the survey area can be either professional targets (software often provides a printable pdf file with various targets automatically recognized during data processing) or clearly visible nails (or stakes). We can recognize these homemade tools by highlighting the top of their surface with a bright colour.

---

[1] Manacorda 2004, p. 108
[2] Mickel 2015
[3] A recent paper by Prins (Prins 2016) quantifies the metric accuracy of the traditional field surveying method at around 8-10 centimetres, i.e. as much as a medium-sized pebble. Although this quantification is useful to provide the order of magnitude of this error, clearly cannot be generalized.
[4] Chiabrando et al. 2010

This information, that will be inserted in post-production into the model, allows for geo-referencing, i.e. placing the model in its real position. This, when it is subsequently integrated with GIS software, allows for the production of any spatial analysis.

To assure a correct colour reading, a colour checker in the scene can be added. This generally presents all photos homogeneously, producing even more realistic models.

With this procedure the SfM models offer an accuracy of between 6 and 10 mm. Such an accurate survey allows us to extract a very large amount of information, including 2D ortho-photos (from which it is possible to produce traditional architectural plans by tracing walls and features) but more importantly 3D results – that can be adapted to specific research and archive needs. The software offers the possibility to automatically extract profiles from the 3D model, thus having plans and sections of the excavation area necessary at the time of the study for *posteriori*, use, including cuts at centimetre distance. This allows for the documentation in great detail of items without being constrained by their position during the excavation.[5].

The key aspects of experimenting with 3D documentation to develop its application for archaeological excavation and architectural structures can be briefly summarized in:

- faithful rendering of the excavation/structure/monument in its three dimensions;
- elimination of subjectivity in the planimetric representation of the stratigraphic deposit;
- speed of acquisition;
- measurability of the excavation/structure/monument in its three spatial dimensions (X, Y, Z);
- integration of 3D information with 2D information (plans);
- geo-referencing of the survey;
- ease of reading three-dimensional data;
- completeness of the survey.

Unlike traditional excavation surveying, the use of 3D surveying techniques eliminates subjectivity, as well as significantly reduces errors, thus obtaining a level of detail that does not require choices or selection of information a priori and achieving a completely objective recording of the data with a real and faithful representation.[6]. (Figure 11)

2.2 Excavation of San Biagio in Venella

During 2015, in order to restart the investigations in the area of the archaic sanctuary known as S. Biagio alla Venella, from the homonymous small church that dominates the area, the Superintendence of Archaeology of Basilicata established a working group which including

prof. Carlo Rescigno (University of Campania Luigi Vanvitelli – S. Maria Capua Vetere), dr. Andrea D'Andrea (Interdepartmental Centre of the University of Oriental Studies of Naples), prof. Angela Pontrandolfo, prof. Luca Cerchiai and prof. Fausto Longo (University of Salerno)[7].

The sanctuary of San Biagio alla Venella is situated approx. 6.6 km from Metaponto, on a slope that descends eastwards towards the Avinella valley, a tributary waterway of the Basento. From the top of the hill on which the modern church of San Biagio is situated, it is possible to see, beyond the river, the plateau of San Teodoro – Incoronata, just 2.5 km away. Despite having played a crucial role in defining the history of the territorialisation of the Metapontine colony, the sanctuary of San Biagio has remained substantially unpublished. It is, above all, devoid of any in-depth study of its topographical reconstruction and building phases. The oldest study dates back to the end of the 7th century BC and the beginning of the following one. The new study on S. Biagio alla Venella required a specific activity dedicated to the reconstruction of the geo-morphological outline of the area in which the structures of the sanctuary are distributed. This activity aims to propose a new plan of the ruins that are still visible and to reassess, in a timely manner, the building and monumental history of the sacred area.

D. Adamesteanu in 1973 and M.L. Nava in 1999 provide some plans without reference to the morphology of the places (Figure 12). M. Torelli[8] and F. De Stefano[9] resumed the previous cartography without making any substantial changes. L. Giardino, illustrated the phase of abandonment of the sanctuary and the plant of a Hellenistic age farm[10].

The remains of the archaeological structures rise in the centre of the small valley that characterizes the area. The area, at the time of the latest survey of activities, was greatly affected by the previous excavations, which had profoundly changed the treading quotas. This made it difficult to interpret the remains (Figure 13).

Therefore, a first, fundamental intervention was the systematization of the past available graphic documentation. This provided a general digital plan of the site with the correct positioning of the objects and structures.

In the 1970s, during the explorations conducted by Adamesteanu, a 10 x 10 m grid was physically drawn on the ground with lime. This is evidenced by a photo found in the archive. Subsequently, this partition was taken up and extended by De Siena in the 1990s to cover the remains of the Hellenistic farm, which had emerged at the time.

---

[5] Prins 2016
[6] Campana, Francovich 2007

[7] The excavation campaign, held that same year, was conducted by Dr. Teresa Cinquantaquattro (at that time superintendent of the Archaeological Superintendence of Basilicata) and Prof. Carlo Rescigno; coordinated, for aspects related to digital and instrumental survey, by Andrea D'Andrea, Rosario Valentini and the writer.
[8] Torelli 2011
[9] De Stefano 2014 e 2016
[10] Giardino 2012, p. 607, fig. 33

Figure 11. Example of 3D stratigraphy (Seglamien excavation by University of Naples L'Orientale – Courtesy of Marco Barbarino)

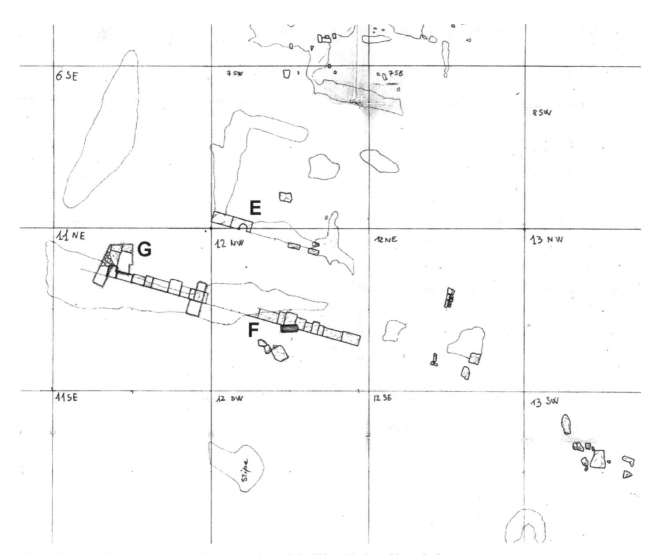

Figure 12. One of the paper plans of the excavations of the '70s with the grid marked.

Figure 13. Satellite view of the archaeological area of San Bagio alla Venella, from Google Earth.

Unfortunately, no pegs belonging to these grids was found in situ. We therefore relied on the visible archaeological structures and the few overall plans of the area, using them as reference points, to digitally report the numerous plans of individual buildings, deposits and tombs found in the archive. The operation was rather laborious considering the different scales and supports on which these graphic representations were drawn up.

This work finally provided a complete vision of the archaeological context, returning to their correct position the various discoveries made over the years. This information was subsequently linked to the topographic polygonal which was specially created by a team of the University "L'Orientale" and the writer during activities of the 2015 mission.

Once the analysis, recovery and positioning of the previous graphic documentation were completed, we created a topographic polygonal on the ground with 7 vertices outside the archaeological area. The cornerstones were then geo-referenced with GPS in differential mode. The new excavation, were thus correctly positioned in the new digital cartography. This new dig took place during the investigations of 2015 and 2017.

Despite, the collected and systematized documentation, this only reflected the situation at the planimetric level of the area. It had a lack of information on the volumes of the structures (e.g. there were no sections in any of the survey).

Therefore, a series of 3D surveys were performed using some of the most recent technologies available.

The new complete survey of the area (Figure 14) was aimed at providing both valid spatial references on which to anchor the plan (obtained from the digitization of the various paper plans of the archive) San Biagio has terraces and slopes almost certainly connected with the cultural practices of the sanctuary. Therefore, it is key a survey that makes immediately readable the height jumps and paths. This allows for the correct interpretation of the function of the structures found which is an undoubtedly valuable tool for the archaeologist.

For the 3D survey a FARO FOCUS 3D X130 was used, setting the geometric resolution to 1/5, the dot quality to 1/4 and the zenith weighted colour balance. Nineteen scans were performed with resolution, based on the selected parameters, is below the centimetre (7 mm) at 10 meters, while the quality value ensures less noise and therefore a greater number of reliable points for each cloud. The instrument used has a camera at 70 MPx so, beyond the geometric information, the RGB colour data was also acquired allowing to return a cloud of coloured points. The acquisition took only one day of work.

During the acquisition all the sensors were activated on the instrument, i.e. GPS, compass, altimeter and inclinometer. This facilitated the alignment of the individual scans during processing.

The alignment was carried out using SCENE software. The clouds were processed (filtered and cleaned) and recorded; at the end of the alignment operations there was an average error of 7 mm.

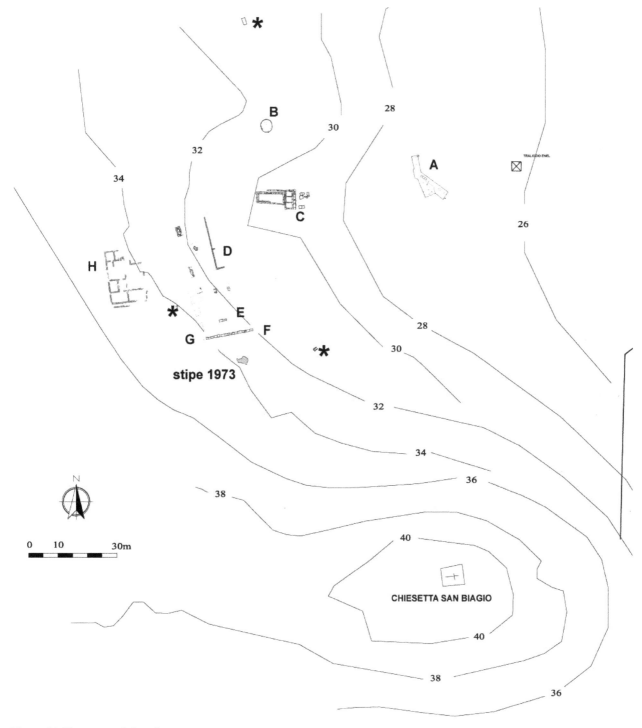

Figure 14. New general site plan.

The final point cloud (Figure 15) was subsequently used to extract new cartographic information such as the DTM of the area, the plan and section of the various structures surveyed. The post-processing was performed with the JRC 3D Reconstructor software, which cuts the cloud to the desired level and obtains polylines that followed exactly the profiles of the selected points as well as sections of the cloud with desired metric intervals (e.g. cuts every 20 or 50 cm). Overlapping these curves (which can be exported in DXF format in a CAD environment) provided very detailed plans and sections.

The plan obtained from the 3D model was superimposed on the archaeological plan created by the vectorization of the archive plans. Inevitably there were some deviations and inaccuracies, mainly due to problems related to a vectorization of not homogenous graphic material, at different scales and on supports often irregular for traditional scanning. Errors in positioning of the monuments were higher than the geometry of the single evidences[11].

---

[11] In some cases, it was not possible to make a precise overlap because the remains identified did not correspond to previous reproduction. This is because certain parts were damaged or eroded due to the passage of time.

Figure 15. The archaeological area of S. Biagio alla Venella from the cloud of laser scanner points. The image shows the morphological trend of the place.

Figure 16. View from above of the model obtained by terrestrial photogrammetry of the Fountain of the site of S. Biagio alla Venella.

Although the laser scanner survey was extremely valid (from a metric point of view) and advantageous (from the point of view of acquisition time), the result in terms of graphic resolution is not sufficient for a detailed analysis of individual structures. For this reason, a close-range photogrammetric survey of the individual buildings was carried out.

The photographic shots were taken at an average distance of about 2 meters from the structures. This obtained a final pixel resolution of less than one centimetre. A resolution that ensured a high definition of the final image, allowing a clear view of the building materials and their state of conservation. Figure 16 shows the degree of photorealistic detail attained with the terrestrial photogrammetric survey.

The 2015 surveys included in-depth field studies with some excavations in areas considered strategic for a

better understanding of the site. One of these areas, located at about 20 m from the krene, at a slightly higher altitude, hosts a circular furnace already identified by Adamesteanu excavations. The archaeologist believed it could be the production area of architectural coroplastics or clay statuettes[12] of the archaic age sanctuary. The new excavation of 2015 noted that the site has never been fully explored.

Although the new investigations did not fully reveal the structure, the firing chamber (with a diameter of approx. 4.14 x 3.76 m) was examined. The firing chamber is covered with the same layer of concocted clay and has approx. 1.40 m in height. The opening to the feeding chamber (not yet explored) is to the south and lines blocks

---

[12] Adamesteanu 1964

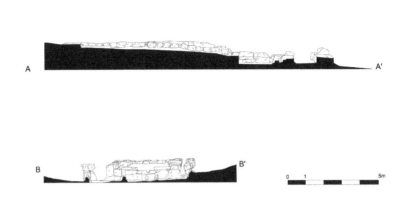

Figure 17. Sections of the basin obtained from the photogrammetric survey.

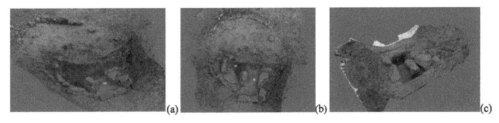

Figure 18. Snapshot of photogrammetric survey of the furnace in two different excavation periods (a) e (b) in the first phase and (c) in the last phase.

with reuse invitingly. Given the size, type of structure and constructive details, we assume a chronology far posterior to that indicated by Adamesteanu.

The second trench was carried out to the west of the structure F and identified a discharge of materials distributed along the entire east strip. The numerous materials found (including *sime*, drips and archaic coroplastics) have provided further information, useful to define chronological ranges and religious functions.

We used close – range photogrammetry with total station support to document the trenches, in particular, the furnace (a piece with due to narrow spaces was delicate to excavate).

The 3D survey has the added value, providing the basis for an evolutive comparison of different methodological approaches. The integration of data guarantees the correct visualization of the information acquired at different times. Moreover, it develops a system that can enhance old and new survey methods to improve the entire spatial information.

2.3 The project "Ancient Appia Landscapes"

The *Ancient Appia Landscapes* (AAL)® project was started by the Department of Cultural Heritage Sciences of the University of Salerno in 2011. It was directed by Professor Alfonso Santoriello, in collaboration with the then archaeological Superintendence of Salerno, Avellino, Benevento and Caserta[13] and the Archaeology Laboratory "M. Napoli".

[13] With the sponsorship of the IMAA-CNR of Tito Scalo (Pz), the GeoGisLab of the Department of Biosciences and Territory of the University of Molise, the Department of Science and Technology of the University of Sannio, and the endorsement of the National Union of Italian Pro Loco (UNPLI). Santoriello 2017.

The aim of the research is to study the route of the Via Appia in the ancient area of *Beneventum*. The ultimate goal is the identification of the phenomena that influenced the settlement dynamics in this area, both before and after the construction of the consular road.[14].

The project has already achieved two important objectives: i) it enabled the definition of the archaeological map of the town of Benevento, and ii) it allowed to make new hypotheses on the route of the ancient Appia.

Data collected as part of the last survey campaign (July 2017), allowed the identification of some sections of the Appian way as part of the road network still used nowadays.

The area of interest is located between the town of Benevento, the Hyrpinian Apennines and the Calore River. It is located on a series of wide alluvial areas close to the basin into which the rivers Sabato and Calore flow.[15]

Notably, two sites have been found, identifiable with the toponyms mentioned in the 'Tabula Peutingeriana', i.e. *ad Calorem*, not so far from Ponte Rotto. This is an important bridge of the imperial age located ten miles from Benevento and used to cross the Calore in the direction of *Aeclanum*, and *Nuceriola* (or *Nucriola*), in Masseria Grasso.

In this area a road section was brought to light. This is approximately 14 meters long and 5.6 meters wide. Findings from the most ancient stratigraphies allow to date it back to the end of the 4th and the beginning of the 3rd century B.C. (probably in connection with the foundation of the Latin colony *Beneventum* in 268 B.C.). Moreover, the repeated maintenance interventions testify its use at least until late antiquity.[16]

Research performed in the areas crossed by the *Via Appia* is strongly multidisciplinary. It is also characterized by a series of specific phases of study ranging from archival research to the use of the most modern technologies.

Access to publicly available archaeological data from historical archives combined with the retrieval of historical maps and aerial photographs allowed to conduct a geomorphological study – this was crucial to understand the formation processes of local and regional stratification.

Geomagnetic (GM) terrestrial surveys provided extensive knowledge of buried features on a large scale. Ground Penetrating Radar (GPR) enabled detailed planning of archaeological excavations. The overlap between archaeological datasets and geophysical surveys also allowed the identification of the route of the ancient *Via Appia* near the town of Benevento and the identification of the archaeological site of *Nuceriola*. Areas with significant

Figure 19. View of the excavation in the Masseria Grasso site, July 2017 (courtesy of prof. A. Santoriello)

anomalies in terms of archaeological evidence have been studied through *infrasite* surveys using a sampled collection of surface artifacts and non-invasive geophysical techniques. This allowed to obtain high-resolution images of the subsoil. The related geomagnetic measurements were performed using an optical pumped magnetometer G-858 while the GPR profiles were performed by the Subsurface Interface Radar (SIR 3000 GSSI).[17]

The interventions of preventive archaeology conducted by the University of Salerno allowed the recovery of new archaeological data. Such data, together with an intense inspection activity, have allowed the definition of an archaeological map in GIS environment. The systematic surveys were planned following a reasoned sampling based on the road layout hypotheses identified in previous studies. The surveys included systematic-intensive criteria, supported by the GPS survey of each Topographical Unit [UT]. Road layout hypotheses were mainly based on the works of Meomartini in the early 1900s and those of Quilici in the early 1990s.[18]

The identification, collection, integration and ongoing management of natural and anthropic datasets (geomorphological, archeo-morphological and from surface collection) provided predictive scenarios of the processes that have conditioned the settlement and productive dynamics of the place.[19]

In 2015, the assessment of an anomaly found in some geophysical surveys led to the identification of a production area situated north-west of the road. This was also confirmed during the subsequent excavation campaign in July 2016. (Figure 19)

The production area was divided into different environments and working areas. Two '*furnaces*' have

[14] De Vita, Terribile 2016
[15] Santoriello 2017.
[16] Tomay *et al.* 2012.

[17] Rizzo *et al.* (in press).
[18] Santoriello, Rossi 2016
[19] De Vita, Terribile 2016

been identified with certainty and the presence of a third one is deemed very likely. The stratigraphic analysis found high quantity of ceramic material, fragmentary but with completely re-constructible shapes (e.g. thin walls), and also numerous elements with evident firing defects or processing waste. This allowed dating the ceramic production activity between the Augusteo-Tiberian age and the middle of the 1st century AD.

In addition to traditional excavation documentation, 3D surveying methods such as terrestrial and aerial photogrammetry were used. The choice of these methods was made with the aim of obtaining expeditious but highly accurate surveys. This, indeed, would guarantee a total coverage of the excavation area without the risk of losing information due to inevitable simplifications – typical of traditional two-dimensional surveys. This would also allow the extraction of a considerable mass of data, whose information could be systematized with past and future data.

The implementation of innovative systems applied to archaeological research is consistent with the process of 'rejuvenation' and involvement of the user. Indeed, this is based through an accessible and convenient communication of information to the public, which characterizes the AAL.[20].

The 3D survey methodology perfectly fits into the routine of the archaeological excavation. A topographic network was set up on the site using a differential GPS from TOPCON. The same instrumentation was used to acquire the absolute coordinates of some nails positioned along the edges of the excavation. These nails (clearly identifiable on the ground also thanks to a bright colouring that characterize the heads) were systematically acquired, as ground control points (GCPs) from photographs taken for the purpose of three-dimensional restitution. In this way it was possible to establish the scale and geo-reference the three-dimensional model, consistent, and therefore comparable with the other information collected (such as maps and geophysical analyses).

A Samsung compact camera mounted on a topographic pole and remotely controlled via an app was used for the acquisition.

Photographic shots were done to cover the entire excavation area each time and, thus, to obtain faithful reproductions of the entire excavation in all its phases. Orthophotos, sections, DEM and contour lines (namely elevations) were extracted from these reproductions.

From the high-resolution orthophotos (Figure 20) it was possible to extract detailed plans of the different excavation phases.

The material was then inserted into a GIS system specifically created for the management of the data of the entire research.[21]

Among the various analyses, particularly interesting was the comparison between the photogrammetric survey and the results of geo-radar prospecting at different acquisition quotas. Integration and comparison of different information allowed the interpretation of the anomalies reported by the geophysical surveys (Figure 21).

This also allowed to plan and broaden the scope of the 2017 excavation campaign.

---

[20] Santoriello 2017b

[21] De Vita, Terribile 2016

Figure 20. Orthophoto of the 2016 survey (view from the top)

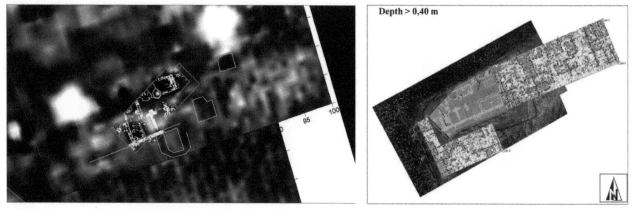

Figure 21. Integration of orthophoto from 3D survey, the resulting vector planimetry, and results from geophysical survey (by courtesy of Prof. Alfonso Santoriello)

3

Requalification and Enhancement

Article 6 of the Cultural Heritage Code states: "Enhancement consists in the exercise of the functions and in the regulation of activities aimed at promoting knowledge of the cultural heritage and at ensuring the best conditions for the public use and enjoyment of the heritage itself . . .".

To date the debate on the Enhancement of cultural heritage is very open among Italian scholars. A brilliant synthesis is offered by Carlo Pavolini in his recent book[1], citing the positions of some of the most active participants in this national (Italian) debate.

The concept of valorisation can be defined as the set of practices that increase the value that a good (e.g. a museum, an archive or a library) can offer to the community, and that make this fruitful, through management and promotion. When it comes to cultural heritage the concept of valorisation is not limited to the monetary aspect. A museum able to generate not only income, but also higher visibility and participation from the community can be considered "valorised", even if it does not reach the break-even point. This is because it stimulates the community to wonder and re-consider its own history. It follows that to be valorised a museum, an archive or a library must first be accessible, known and functional to research and production of culture.

According to the Italian law, are part of the cultural heritage "immovable and movable objects which, according to articles 10 and 11 of Cultural Heritage and Landscape Code, are of artistic, historical, archaeological, ethno-anthropological, archival and bibliographical interest [. . .]". Are part of the landscape heritage, instead, "real properties and areas indicated in article 134, constituting expression of the historical, cultural, natural, morphological and aesthetic values of a territory, [. . .]".

Publicly owned cultural heritage assets are intended for use by the community, compatibly with its preservation and institutional use.

Making an asset accessible, however, is not sufficient to enhance its value. Actually, the wrong type of access to monuments or museums can even damage the "value", as well as undermine its meaning.

The rapid evolution of technologies and tools for 3D surveying has revolutionized the field of cultural heritage enhancement. Various open virtual heritage applications have proved to be effective tools for cultural fruition. Indeed, they allowed the combination of the most classic communication systems with educational 3D movies in computer graphics, but also projections and holographs, serious games, augmented reality apps and participative virtual spaces. These achieved high levels of penetration and engagement among visitors – especially among the youngest.

3.1 3D design of interventions

The preservation of an ancient monument includes both the maintenance of its physical reality and the continuous process of information gathering, study and dissemination of the asset. These are fundamental to a correct understanding of the heritage. In turn, this is key to good planning aimed at protecting and preserving the heritage itself.

Integrated conservation needs appropriate financial resources [2]. Public funding is generally completely absorbed by the huge cost of excavation, conservation and management of the archaeological site. A modern valorisation system should then include the public in the whole process, by also stimulating appreciation for the conservation of the monuments. To this purpose, virtual reconstructions (e.g. 3D models and VR animations) are very effective especially in public presentations or exhibitions.

The cultural information produced in archaeology increasingly ends up on the web in different forms (thematic maps, three-dimensional models, images, articles, etc.), information that the general public can decide to deepen through scientific publications on site and, vice versa, the visitor will be led to deepen the museum contents and to share them socially.

Virtual archaeology means the reproduction of a real object through an interactive simulation. It is called 'augmented reality' because it increases the level of information conveyed electronically, in a way that would not normally be perceivable with the five senses. It requires digital tools such as computers or mobile devices with a compass, GPS location, internet and camera, and can be achieved in several ways:

- by framing a real object with a mobile device to obtain a 3D reconstruction of it

---

[1] Pavolini 2017, pp.115 – 147

[2] Carta Italiana del Restauro.

- by using a mobile application downloadable from the web that allows continuing the museum exploration after the visit, at home
- through natural interaction: body gestures are used to interact with the technology.

The accurate survey of a historical structure, not only provides essential information for research, but it also represents an ideal tool to describe the construction process of the building and to communicate the value and the meaning of this to the community.[3] To do so, the integration of different relevant techniques is often required. These needs be combined in a way that is functional to the design of the interventions[4].

In this new perspective of valorisation, the archaeologist can and must be the first actor, expanding the means and consequently the horizons at his disposal, and being able to overcome those obstacles that his training inevitably poses.

3.2 Torre del Greco, Villa Sora

The seaside *villa* in Contrada Sora (Villa Sora, Torre del Greco, Naples) is now deeply renovated due to the presence, until the 1970s, of modern artefacts built by reusing the elevated parts of the ancient structures[5] (Figure 22). The layout of the villa dates back to the second quarter of the 1st century B.C. due to the presence of paintings of II style and considering that the walls were built using the *opus quasi-reticulatum* technique while the doorframes were built with the *opus vittatatum* one. After 79 A.D. in the same area was also built another building dating back to the IV-VI century A.D. In the 19th century some late burials were found near the villa which testify the presence of a site built after the destruction caused by the Vesuvius.

The area was first discovered at the end of the 18th century. Some excavations took place then to be paused for around 150 years. New excavations were undertaken by M. Pagano over the period 1989-92. These intended to explore the eastern part of the complex. Today, the archaeological site of Villa Sora in Torre del Greco is situated in an extremely difficult and problematic environmental framework, close to the Naples – Salerno coastal railway line which, built in the mid-19th century, seriously damaged the coastal landscape,

Then Villa is also enclosed by the imposing cemetery of Torre del Greco, which looms over the area with its retaining walls. The area is also surrounded by greenhouse crops, shacks and modern ruins. The site is therefore mostly unknown and inaccessible to the general public[6]. Nevertheless, the site is continuously crossed by unauthorized tourists headed to the nearby beach. These use the not so easy to walk way to sea, just in front of the ruins. They way probably follow the ancient private path of the villa (Figure 23).

In the past, the Superintendence, used the limited funds available for the cleaning, basic maintenance, and protection of the area. A more substantial intervention took place in 2008, with the construction of a roof over the frescoed parts and a fence on the west side[7].

In 2015, thanks to an agreement between the University "L'Orientale" of Naples and the Special Superintendence of Pompeii, Herculaneum and Stabia, a project for the requalification of the area was started. This had the aim to use the most innovative acquisition technologies used for Cultural Heritage.

The agreement consisted in systematic study and documentation of the remains of the villa and in the preparatory activity for the elaboration of a more articulated project of excavation, restoration and use of the site. This included:

- the performance of a new 3D survey of the visible structures;
- the production of ortho-photos for the analysis of masonry units, walls and floor decorations;
- the documentation of the state of conservation of the archaeological remains;
- the compilation of stratigraphic data sheets of masonry units, walls and floor coverings.

Therefore, the project was aimed at obtaining a detailed survey of the monument's actual state, with the application of 3D survey techniques and using a digital replica characterized by high resolution and precision. This was to provide updated topographical data of the archaeological area, and adequate support for an in-depth historical and architectural study of the villa.

During the spring of 2015 the Centro Interdipartimentale di Servizi per l'Archeologia (CISA), of the University "L'Orientale" of Naples started the activities included in the collaboration agreement by designing and carrying out the 3D survey with laser scanner of the archaeological evidence still recognizable on the ground. This survey allowed the correct positioning – for the first time in a three-dimensional space – of all the archaeological remains, as well as the possibility of extracting new graphic information (plans, sections and elevations). These proved to be useful to forthcoming field investigations and to the development of a project for the preservation and use of the entire archaeological site.

The survey carried out with the Faro Focus X3D 130 laser scanner, required only one day of field acquisition.

---

[3] Amici 2008
[4] Bitelli *et al.* 2017
[5] Langella 1978
[6] access is allowed on special occasions only to small groups of visitors led by the GAV – (Vesuvius Archaeological Group).

---

[7] Guidobaldi 2015

Figure 22. Remains of modern superimpositions on the structures of the ancient Roman villa.

Figure 23. Location of the Villa Sora site from Google Earth.

To cover the entire area, 27 scans were performed with the instrument acquisition parameters set to obtain accurate and detailed representations of the archaeological information. The survey had to guarantee a high geometric resolution compatible with the purposes of the subsequent architectural restitution.[8].

In spring 2016, after some cleaning and maintenance activities had taken place, a new laser scanner survey was carried out. This was limited to the areas involved by the recent maintenance. The resulting model was superimposed on the previous survey allowing the rapid updating of the plan and sections and most importantly the characterization of the floors, as well as the new areas freed from the deposits of the 79 AD eruption.

What remains of the villa is divided into two main areas. These appear distinct due to a number of anthropic actions over time. The eastern part is covered and fenced since Pagano's excavations because characterized by the presence of narrow rooms with high decorated walls. The western part is wider and uncovered, with only few rows of structures actually preserved. This part has been greatly affected over time by the anthropic action and, consequently, worse preserved (Figure 24).

Due to these 'environmental' reasons, special care was taken in planning and executing the shootings. To ensure the correct alignment of the scans during the recording phase, two different acquisition methods were used. In the covered area, characterized by numerous finely frescoed rooms, five spherical targets were positioned along the walkway at the top of the excavation edge. This was to not hind the decoration and to guarantee visibility in the shots[9];

To capture as much detail as possible, the scanner has been positioned along the platform surrounding the excavation, in every room and along the corridor to the North (Figure 25) in correspondence of two narrow tunnels built in ancient times. These allow to see two rooms not completely brought to light yet.

The scanner settings for more accurate acquisitions with long and tangential connections have been:

- External profile < 20m
- Resolution 1/5
- Quality 3x
- Clean sky and clean edges' filters
- Active inclinometer
- Active compass
- Active Altimeter

Moreover, in the open area the laser scanner sensors have been fully enabled (inclinometer, compass, altimeter and GPS) to ensure a correct automatic recording of point clouds. The total number of shots acquired in this area is the same as in the eastern area although the surface is much larger.

After the shooting took place, two portions of point clouds, one of the west side and one on the east side, were separately processed by eliminating any inconsistent points and by automatically aligning the scans. Then, the two sub-sets of data were associated through the manual recognition of some features in both the clouds. After this, the average alignment error was less than one centimetre. This was compatible with the chosen scale of detail for the final survey of the archaeological structures.[10].

The model allowed the updating the existing planimetry (Figure 27) and provided, for the first time, an overview of the archaeological remains, which on site are difficult to read. The area protected by a roof and surrounded by a fence to protect the decorated environments is completely separate from the uncovered part. This separation, is exacerbated by the presence of a belt of land forming a sort of trench between the two areas, which makes them invisible to each other. Moreover, the real height of walking plane is cannot be discerned.

The virtual reconstruction allowed to remove both the cover and the fence. This enables a complete view (Figure 26) of the ancient environments. Moreover, from the model it was possible to extract plants and elevations that confirmed the existence, between the two zones, of a single ground level (Figure 28).

The detailed survey with the image-based methodology (SfM photogrammetry) has been designed to extract high-definition orthophotos of the walls of different environments. This allowed to document the state of conservation of paintings and wall structures and to provide support for the archaeological cataloguing of the wall stratigraphy.

Over two working days, about 100 photos were captured for each room with a Nikon reflex camera (with no full frame). However, the resolution of the reliefs is still very high, since the shots were taken close to the walls. The poor light conditions made it necessary to use the tripod in some environments. The processing took about a week. The reliefs were georeferenced and made to the relevant scale by using the points extracted directly from the laser survey. In practice, the recognition was based on the laser scans[11], by using the Faro Scene software – mainly based

---

[8] The on-field activities were carried out by Dr. A. D'Andrea, A. Bosco e R. Valentini with the collaboration of F. Forte, M. Fusco, P. Maietta e P. Memoli.

[9] The presence of a structure made of metal beams and of a walkway designed to facilitate the visit of the archaeological remains with a view from above, has allowed positioning the spherical targets for scanning through a magnetic support in several points of the structure.

[10] The laser scanner acquires in scale 1:1. the alignment error of less than one centimeter allows elaborating a very precise survey in scale 1:20 highlighting the construction details and the rooms configuration.

[11] To make the recognition of points easier and more precise, this operation has been carried out by using a "flat view" mode that allows viewing the single scan as a 360° photo. This keeps intact the coordinates and the references with the 3D point cloud. By selecting a precise point, you can get the information linked to it, including the spatial coordinates X, Y, Z.

Figure 24. Photographs of the uncovered area (I) and the covered area (II – III) in Villa Sora.

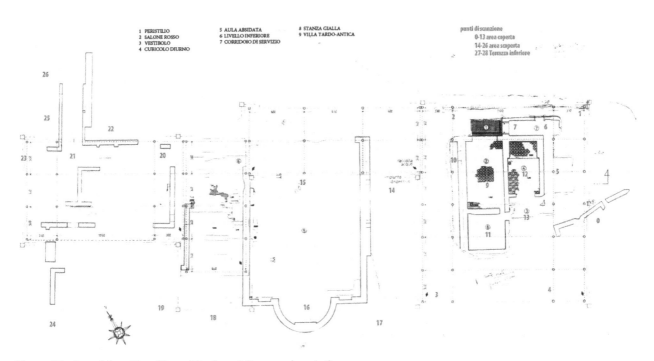

Figure 25. plan of the villa with positioning of the scanning stations.

on points whose spatial coordinates have been extracted. These points were then identified within the photographs taken for the SfM surveys – these were used as markers. This allowed to obtain perfect 3D replicas, metrically accurate and very realistic (Figure 29).

About 40 orthophotos were extracted from these surveys. These provided the basis for the analysis of structural and decorative degradation (Figure 30), according to the best practice used for the Great Pompeii Project (GPP).

As mentioned above, the work was aimed at designing a requalification process that would allow the public to access and enjoy the site. The work was also intended to contribute to the inclusion of the main Vesuvian sites in a tourist route.

The accurate 3D survey provided the support for an adequate planning of the restorations, for the preparation of a new coverage and the identification of tourist route that would facilitate access and, most importantly, the

Figure 26. Aligned laser scanner point cloud.

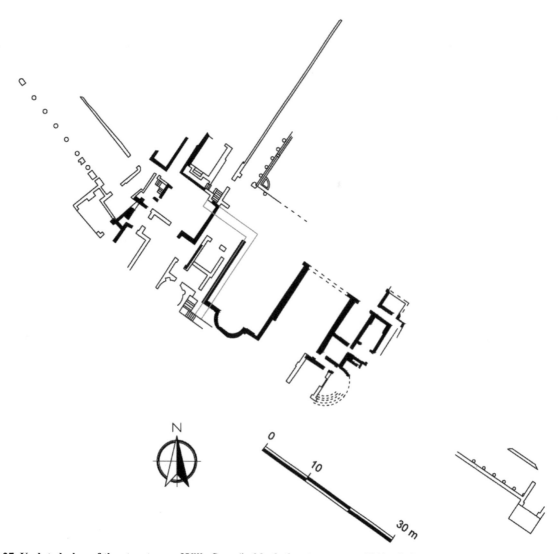

Figure 27. Updated plan of the structures of Villa Sora (in black the structures still '*in situ*').

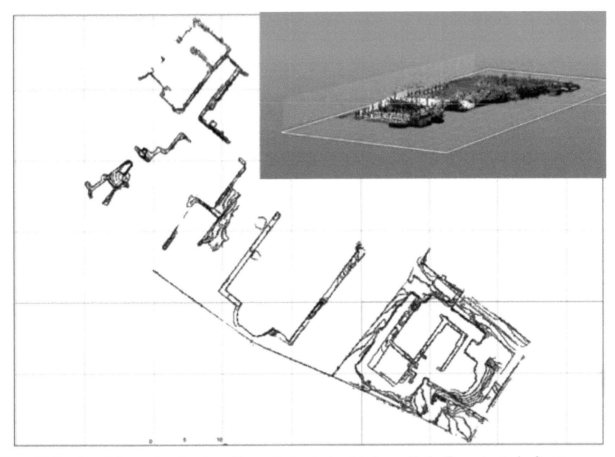

Figure 28. Creation of plans and sections by cutting vertical or horizontal planes with the 'Reconstructor' software.

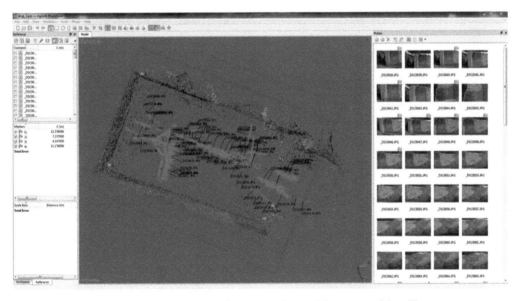

Figure 29. Photoscan elaboration of the photogrammetric survey of one of the rooms of the villa.

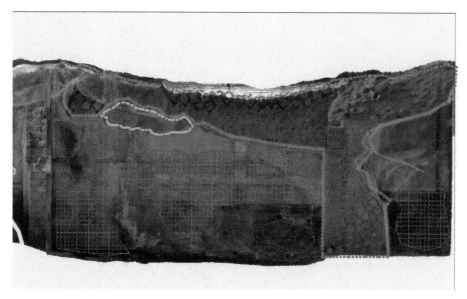

Figure 30. Example of an ortho-photo extracted from the photogrammetric model on which the degradation analysis was inserted by using the CAD software.

Figure 31. Reconstruction of the elevations of the maritime villa in the Sora district made with the Rhinoceros software.

understanding of the site. Last but not least, the models can be reused as a basis for designing a virtual model that virtual visitors can access and use online (Figure 31)..

3.3 The so-called *Augusteum* of Herculaneum

The second case study selected as an example of enhancement is the virtual reconstruction of the so-called *Augusteum* in Herculaneum carried out within the 3DICONS Project. [12].

The monument is not entirely visible and only the south side is partially preserved. The building, explored in the 18th century by the Bourbons, is still largely unknown, 250 years after its discovery.

The identification and function of this structure has been contested since its discovery. Although it is still completely buried by the volcanic layer, the building is known for the tunnels dug by its first excavators.

---

[12] We thank the architect L. Mastursi for kindly providing the CAD model of the building; T.E. Cinquantaquattro, M. Osanna, M.P. Guidobaldi and E. Santaniello for giving permission to make the 3D model of the still visible part of the building. The model has been realized within 3DICONS (www.3dicons-project.eu).

Figure 32. Picture of the four-sided arch belonging to the *Augusteum* building and currently the only visible part to visitors of the Herculaneum Park.

Several researchers[13] have provided their reconstructions based on two plans drawn in the 18th century and some notes taken during its exploration. Archaeologists have focused their research on the architectural elements of the building and its ancient function. The first digital reconstruction[14] was based on the actual measurements of the visible parts, while in 2008 a scale model integrated the architectural structure with statues and frescoes[15].

In order to highlight some controversial parts of the reconstructions, a new 3D survey of the building was then designed using innovative acquisition systems. This has associated to the digital replica metadata that describes the physical object and records all phases from acquisition to data visualization. In literature, the monument is known under different names: Portico, Forum, Basilica; the latest research identifies it as a building linked to the imperial cult, more precisely the *Augusteum* [16], although there is no epigraphic evidence to support this function. The building was studied only thanks to the famous 18th century gallery

system. In 1744 Bardet de Villeneuve, who directed the excavations between 1741 and 1744, designed three floors of the building. Alcubierre had excavated the monument for the first time a few years earlier, in 1739. Bardet's plans probably referred to maps drawn up at the time, but only partially preserved.

This hypothesis is supported by a number of significant inaccuracies[17]. Three drawings represent the structure in its entirety. Two reproduce the monument in a wider context of public buildings, including the theatre. Even at first glance, inaccuracies in the positioning of the buildings are striking: the theatre is rotated 90 °, the porch and facade of the College of Augustals and the so-called Basilica Noniana are too distant from each other and, consequently, from the *decumanus maximus* [18].

Despite the general map being wrong, the drawing of the *Augusteum* is very detailed and accurate. It includes a front view of the western wall of the building (Figure 33).

Between 1750 and 1751 J.-C. Bellicard and C.-N. Cochin visited Herculaneum. In their publication in 1754, there

---

[13] Pagano 1996, Njabjerg 2002, Mastursi 2008, Allroggen-Bedel 2010, Guidobaldi 2012

[14] Najbjerg 2002

[15] Mastursi 2008

[16] Allroggen-Bedel 2008; Pesando 2003; Guidobaldi 2012

[17] Allroggen-Bedel 2010

[18] Najbjerg 2002

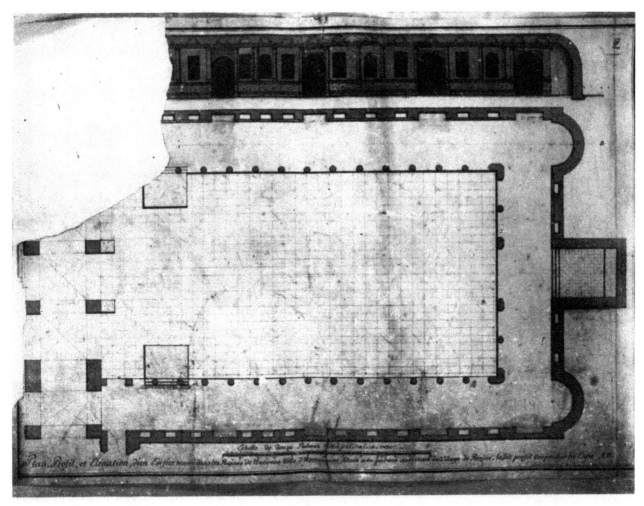

Figure 33. Plan of the *Augusteum* drawn by Bardet de Villeneuve. (From Grell 1982 – https://books.openedition.org/pcjb/docannexe/image/258/img-5.jpg)

is a much more accurate plan of the north-western area of the excavations. There the buildings are placed in a correct spatial relationship. It is likely that the two gentlemen had access to the original excavation plans carried out by de Alcubierre and that not long afterwards they disappeared together with the general plan of the excavations commissioned in 1759 by Weber. An evocative representation of the building is in an engraving made by F. Morghen in 1835[19]. The work is a bird's eye view of the large porticoed building, with some statues inside, including the two equestrian statues of M. Nonius Balbus and his son[20]. The two lateral bases on which the artist places the statues (coming from the public area of the city) are an imagination. When checking the detailed map of Bardet, instead of the bases, there are two small platforms placed against the western and eastern walls of the arcades, accessible by two steps. These platforms were probably courting rather than bases for statues[21]. In the engraving (which represents the building completely excavated) there are some inaccuracies including the long walls.

The map of Bardet (Figure 33) shows a detailed description of the western wall with five large curved niches open at the ground. These are alternating with groups of two or three small arched and rectangular niches. The large niches are surrounded by pilasters with Corinthian capitals and have a filled rectangular space at the top of the arch. In the second niche the inscription is dedicated to the Augustales (CIL X, 977) discovered in 1741 (not in situ). The structure has been revisited by Pagano[22] which provided an axonometric view of the monument. A first complete reconstruction by Najbierg in 1997 was published only afterward[23].

The American researcher mainly focused on the comparison between the 18th century plants with existing remains. He checked the accuracy of the geometry of the ancient drawings, but found the same errors in the reconstruction of the southern part of the monument. Najbjerg published a 3D digital reconstruction of the portico to better analyse the spatial relationship of the building with the opposite Augustal College. The model, unfortunately known only by the pictures included in the publication,

---

[19] The work is currently located in the Royal Palace in Naples.
[20] Allroggen-Bedel 2008
[21] Guidobaldi 2012

[22] Pagano 1996
[23] Najbjerg 2002

is very essential and without any decoration. Thanks to the new relief, Najbjerg identified seven openings in the south façade instead of the five drawn by the Bourbon surveyors.

Based on the reconstruction of Najbjerg, L. Mastursi developed a 1:50 scale model of the building in 2008. He enriched the model by adding the frescoes, statues and other decorative elements from the building, but the correct positioning of the statues is still under discussion. The Bourbons dug many galleries simultaneously in different parts of ancient Herculaneum and often used these galleries several times during the works. Therefore, they did not always correctly record the origin of the found objects[24]. As far as the Basilica is concerned, only a few pieces of data are certainly correct. Inside the central exedra of the north wall of the building, the excavations found a group of imperial marble statues, two of which were seated (Augustus and Claudius) and a third loricate (Titus). Two other statues, representing Augustus and Claudius, were probably on the bases placed in front of the niches. As for the painted walls (promptly detached by the Bourbons), little data is available for a precise repositioning. For example, four large paintings, whose surface is slightly concave, can almost certainly be placed in the two niches at the bottom of the northern wall of the porticoes. All the statues and frescoes are currently kept in the Archaeological Museum of Naples.

The 3D model was built on the basis of the final architectural design elaborated by Mastursi who digitally reproduced the reconstructive hypotheses made by Najbjerg and Pagano. The CAD model was integrated by the 3D survey of the four-sided arch, still visible in the SE corner of the building. This was made with the technique of Close-Range photogrammetry.[25]

The 2D CAD drawing was analysed to verify and correct the geometry (intersections, unions, etc.). Then it was integrated, positioned and rotated to get a better view of the structure in a 3D scene. Thanks to common 3D modelling tools (extrusion, lofts, sweeps, Boolean operations, etc.) it was possible to generate surfaces and solids both for the general structure of the building and the many more detailed decorative elements – namely capitals with acanthus leaves, column bases and altar frames. 2D plans, sections and CAD elevations were also used to support the creation of the building and its correct dimensional, formal and geometric properties. The 3D model of the frescoes and four of the statues originally located inside the *Augusteum* were created using the Structure from Motion photogrammetry technique (Figure 34).

For each statue 150-180 photos were captured and processed in the Photoscan software[26]. Clouds of about 1-2 million points were obtained for each statue. The point clouds were cleaned to remove scattered points caused by the "noise" of the photographs, due to the imperfect lighting inside the museum. They were also resized through some reference targets positioned in the scene. A 3D polygonal model (mesh) was generated for each statue built from the dense point clouds. The surface of the polygonal models (over 5 million faces) was checked and modified to remove the remaining noise (self-intersecting triangles, non-manifold faces, etc.). This was due to interpolation error as we had decimated to produce models lighter than about 20,000 faces.

The procedure was also used for the four-sided arch. In this case, some sights were placed on the structure whose coordinates were acquired with the help of the total station. These points were used to optimize the 3D reconstruction and provide the final model with real measurements. Finally, a dense point cloud of about 7 million points and mesh of 12 million faces was obtained. A decimation process was also performed for the statues in Geomagic Studio software establishing a maximum tolerance. This limit was set at 4 cm for the porch and 0.5 cm for the statues.

All 3D models were then imported into Rhinoceros to integrate the CAD model with the statues and the four-sided model. Rhinoceros uses a modelling approach based on NURBS (non-uniform rational base spline), suitable when the model development elements are represented by section lines and can easily handle the entire structure of a CAD format. The integration of the reconstructed model with the four-fronted model was based on the alignment of the parts on common elements. This alignment allowed us to observe a difference of about 20 cm on the horizontal plane and 30 cm in height between the two models (Figure 35).

With not enough information about the surface of the monument, we applied white marble and white plaster to the reconstructive model to obtain a realistic effect. According to the literature, the frescoes were placed in the two apses by texturing the surfaces (Figure 36). Therefore, we then added a tiled roof for the peristyle to have a complete representation of the building.

3D models of the so-called Basilica are available free of charge on the Europeana website. You can find different objects: the CAD model, the replicas of the four imperial statues, the four-fronted, and the complete integration of all the models made. To facilitate sharing and interaction, all 3D models are in 3D PDF format, but the high-resolution model (.ply or .obj) can be provided on request[27].

---

[24] Torelli 2004

[25] D'Andrea *et al.* 2017

[26] The software recently changed its name to Agisoft Metashape (https://www.agisoft.com).

[27] http://www.europeana.eu; https://classic.europeana.eu/portal/et/record/2048703/object_HA_847.html?utm_source=new-website&utm_medium=button

A video of the virtual reconstruction is available at this link: http://vast-lab.org/3dicons/1770.mp4 (Last visit 30/05/2022)

Figure 34. Details of the 3D models of the statues of Claudius and Augustus sitting.

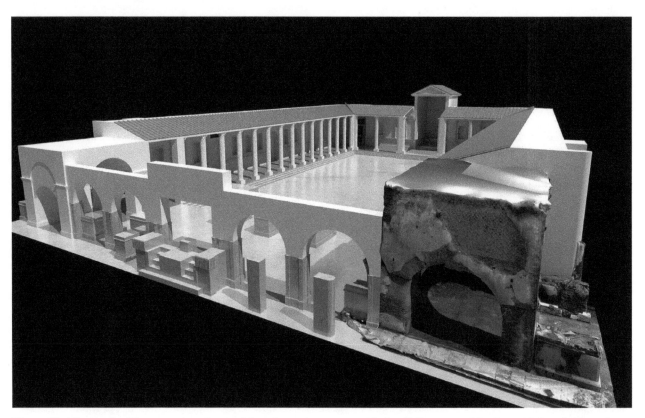

Figure 35. Alignment of the reconstructive model on the vector survey with the SfM survey of the four-sided arch (the only visible part of the monument).

Metadata has enriched digital objects (Figure 37). The increase in freely accessible and downloadable online 3D objects will encourage scholars to reuse these digital objects and better analyse virtual reconstructions in detail. This approach will probably restore the original meaning and spirit of Virtual Archaeology, seen as a cognitive laboratory used by archaeologists to formulate and visualize different and alternative hypotheses. Thanks to this approach, virtual archaeology is archaeology and not simple acquisition and processing of 3D data.

Figure 36. Detail of the north wall of the reconstructive model with inserted frescoes and digital copies of the statues now kept at MANN.

Figure 37. Example of metadata for 3D four-sided arch in Herculaneum from Europeana.

4

Conservation and Preventive Maintenance

Conservation and preventive maintenance of monuments and sites is gradually emerging through case-studies as a way to improve heritage preservation. The UNESCO Chair on Preventive Conservation, Monitoring and Maintenance of Monuments and Sites (PRECOM³OS)[1] was inaugurated in Leuven on 24 March 2009. This has stimulated research and collaboration to understand the nature of preventive conservation for built heritage. These exchanges help to gradually gain a better understanding of the nature and benefits of preventive conservation[2].

Scheduled maintenance activities vary depending on the operating intensity in:

- prevention activities, i.e. activities that do not directly involve the asset. These include both management and maintenance activities aimed at controlling or reducing risk due to the surrounding conditions;
- direct activities on the asset with preventive effectiveness, i.e. preventive activities providing considerable effectiveness in controlling degrading actions with minimal invasiveness;
- protection activities, i.e. direct activities aimed at providing additional resources to the building and its components, such as structural reinforcements, surface protective layers, new technological element etc. . . .;
- maintenance activities, which directly involve the material of the building and are essential to slow down or contain the progression of damage. These activities are designed and carried out with the aim of repairing damage and removing its cause, where possible[3].

Similarly, to preventive medicine practices, the preventive conservation of monuments and sites can be defined by three classes of prevention:

- primary prevention, avoiding the causes of the undesirable effect;
- secondary prevention, for early detection of the symptoms of side effects;
- tertiary prevention, for preventing spread of the undesirable effects or generation of new undesirable effects.

The conservation of built heritage is 'planned and preventive' when it is a long-term process. In addition to the above-mentioned prevention, it is also based on research carried out for museums and collections[4].

This leverages of the concept of risk management where every intervention is part of a long-term process necessary to maintain tomorrow what we are restoring today.

Beyond the degradation analysis typical of restoration, the conservation of the built heritage should also consider the material survey and the study of i) structural behaviour, ii) the resistant sections, iii) of any subsidence and iv) deformations.

Consistently with this, recent codes deal with the assessment and reduction of seismic risk of cultural heritage. The knowledge of the historical construction becomes, therefore, a fundamental prerequisite for both a reliable evaluation of the current seismic safety and the choice of an effective strengthening intervention. The 'knowledge' of the building, for these purposes, is identified as a numerical factor adjusting the mechanical properties of the materials or, alternatively, the relevant seismic action. For example, the 'confidence factor' (Fc), ranges between 1 and 1.35 and affects the reliability of the structural analysis model and the evaluation of the seismic safety index[5].

It can be calculated as the sum of partial confidence factors associated to each investigation category and the related level of depth for the assessment of these. This is:

$$Fc= k + Fc1 + Fc2 + Fc3 + Fc4$$

Where:

k = is a constant value
Fc1= Geometric survey
Fc2= Material survey of construction details
Fc3= Mechanical properties of materials
Fc4= Soil and foundations

As far as the Fc1 factor is concerned, the regulatory standards require the instrumental monitoring of crack patterns, when these involve the geometrical control of the entire construction. This "can be performed by means of topographic, photogrammetric survey procedures, or by using innovative techniques, such as the point cloud generated by the laser scanner".

---

[1] https://set.kuleuven.be/rlicc/research/precomos
[2] Van Balen 2015
[3] Cecchi, Gasparoli 2010
[4] Staniforth 2013

[5] See "Guidelines for the assessment and reduction of seismic risk of the cultural heritage with reference to the Technical Standards for construction in the Decree of the Ministry of Infrastructure and Transport of 14 January 2008".

Geometrical survey	Complete geometrical survey	$F_{C1} = 0.05$
	Complete geometrical survey, with cracking and deformation pattern restitution	$F_{C1} = 0$
Identification of historical and constructive aspects of the construction	Hypothetic identification of constructive phases based on a limited material survey and constructive elements identification together with the comprehension of transformative phases (documental and thematic investigations)	$F_{C2} = 0.12$
	Partial identification of constructive phases and structural behaviour interpretation based on (a) limited material survey and constructive elements identification together with the comprehension of transformative phases (documental and thematic investigations, with diagnostic checks of historiography hypotheses); (b) extensive material survey and constructive elements identification together with the comprehension of transformative phases (documental and thematic investigations)	$F_{C2} = 0.06$
	Complete identification of constructive phases and structural behaviour interpretation based on exhaustive material survey and constructive elements identification together with the comprehension of transformative phases (documental and thematic investigations, with potential diagnostic investigations).	$F_{C2} = 0$
Mechanical properties of materials	Mechanical properties obtained by available data	$F_{C3} = 0.12$
	Limited investigations on mechanical properties	$F_{C3} = 0.06$
	Extensive investigations on mechanical properties	$F_{C3} = 0$
Soil and foundations	Limited investigations on soil and foundations, without geotechnical data and without foundation information	$F_{C4} = 0.06$
	Limited investigations on soil and foundations, with geotechnical data and with foundation information	$F_{C4} = 0.03$
	Extensive investigations on soil and foundations	$F_{C4} = 0$

Figure 38. Definition of the different in-depth levels of investigation on the different aspects of knowledge and related partial confidence factors (as provided by the Italian guidelines).

4.1 Maintenance of complex sites

Which professionalism should be involved in the 'archaeology of the built ' or in the study of ancient monuments, it is not yet clear-cut. The activity involves knowledge of engineering, architecture and, last but not least, archaeology. As it often happens, collaboration is the perfect compromise, but the results are valuable only if each specific field of work is well defined. The risk is that only certain aspects will be dealt with, when there is no general understanding of the construction.

Some suggest that only an experienced archaeologist, with specific expertise in the analysis of ancient buildings and construction techniques, can successfully perform the study of monuments by extracting all possible meanings in their cultural context and thus making them a primary source of information.[6]

The Great Pompeii Project (GPP) is probably the best-known preventive maintenance project in the archaeological field. This project was approved in 2012 by both the European Commission and the Italian government with funding for 105 million euros. The Ministry of Cultural Heritage, Activities & Tourism has developed an action plan inspired by planning and integration criteria that aim to systematically address the problems of conservation and enhancement of the archaeological area.

The GPP is an ambitious scheme based on six plans, i.e. security, works, knowledge, 'capacity building', communication and fruition. This is unsurprising considering that, as expected, all these aspects characterize a site as complex as the one of Pompeii. One of the main objectives is to solve the issue of conservation, to be addressed by adopting an approach of extensive and detailed knowledge of the risks for the systematic planning of conservation interventions and the management of periodic interventions.

In particular, the Knowledge Plan allows continuous monitoring of the site and of the state of conservation of the structures thanks to a specific computer system. Moreover, it is aimed at planning and carrying out all the consolidation and restoration work necessary for the prevention of collapses, in an effective and timely manner.

The GPP applies a methodology already experimented in the context of specific interventions in the archaeological areas of Rome, Ostia Antica and Pompeii itself[7]. It provides for the survey and collection of all the data related to the different aspects of the archaeological structures, linked to both monitoring and conservation

---

[6] Amici 2008

[7] Cecchi, Gasparoli 2010

and to scientific and archival issues (past and future). All this information is preparatory to the design of the interventions to be carried out for each *domus*.

The Knowledge Plan is divided into three operational activities:

* survey, investigation and diagnosis of the structures in the entire built-up area;
* diagnostic surveys and studies for the mitigation of hydrogeological risk;
* design of the priority interventions.

Cataloguing, surveys, investigations and diagnoses for the analytical identification of structural and restoration criticalities were carried out for all the *domus* (c. 1,500) and infrastructures of the ancient city (including walls, roads and funerary complexes). The project was divided into six lots (more or less coinciding with the main *regiones* of the ancient city). Given the complexity of the site (242,000 m^2 of wall surfaces, 17,777 m^2 of paintings, 20,000 m^2 of plaster, 12,000 sqm. of floors and 20,000 sqm. of roofing), the most modern and innovative acquisition and diagnostic technologies were used to obtain this information[8].

In particular, numerous monuments (in some cases entire *insulae*) have been acquired by laser scanner in order to obtain a three-dimensional geo-referenced model of the structures. In many cases this method was necessary due to the criticalities presented by some environments (e.g. hypogeal or not easily accessible environments).

The plan included a survey of vertical surfaces based on orthorectified photography. In this case, however, given the extremely difficulty working conditions – due, for example, to narrow environments and considerably high walls –the plan also required the application of 3D photogrammetric surveys from which high resolution orthophotos were extracted. These would allow the identification of any type of degradation (structural or surface).

The Knowledge Plan allowed obtaining an updated geo-referenced survey on a scale of 1:50 (the previous one was on a scale of 1:500). This allowed the accurate mapping of any degradation (e.g. gaps, cracks, misalignments, etc.), but also of masonry techniques, roofs or furnishing objects. All information has been included (as shapefile) in the dedicated Web-GIS that allows real-time monitoring and design of interventions and periodic inspections.

Therefore, the GPP was the tool that brought the Pompeii site back to modernity, making it a field of experimentation and innovation after being a symbol of degradation and mismanagement[9].

Nevertheless, another important Vesuvian site was at the forefront of scheduled maintenance, already before GPP.

The excavations of Herculaneum, surrounded by the modern town, have addressed big conservation challenges, since always. Indeed, the Herculaneum Conservation Project (HCP) has been devoted to the archaeological site of Herculaneum since 2001. It is an initiative of the Packard Humanities Institute carried out by its operational arm in Italy – the Packard Institute for Cultural Heritage Foundation together with the Herculaneum Archaeological Park[10].

The program is aimed at protecting, enhancing and managing the site of Herculaneum and promoting dissemination and integration with the surrounding community.

The HCP, represents a positive example of public-private partnership for the protection of cultural heritage, able to bring together, in a successful organisation, public officials of the relevant protection authority and specialists in cultural heritage. The private partner, far from taking the place of the public body, supports it with both financial resources and intellectual, professional and organizational resources.

In 2010, the collapse of the *Schola armaturarum* brough to the attention the maintenance problems of the complex site of Pompeii. Hence, the HCP was invited, at the end of 2011, at the General Directorate for Antiquities, to present the example of the conservation and management program of Herculaneum in order to share the lessons learned in a decade of activity with colleagues facing similar challenges.

In particular, the interest was in the GIS data management system created for the Herculaneum site, which had been explicitly mentioned to the Superintendence as a model to be followed also in Pompeii for the excellent results.[11].

The challenge of the project was to guarantee the safety of the buildings to allow the access first of the technicians working on their restoration and conservation and then to the wider public. Therefore, the starting point was the conception of parallel campaigns of ordinary and extraordinary maintenance combining the complex interventions with the standard and the simplest ones. These had the additional goal to progressively the conservation conditions of the site in a staged manner.[12]

The HCP data management system allowed constant monitoring of the maintenance against the recurrence of degradation, and the management of emergency safety measures that enable the public to access the facilities, while waiting for ad hoc funding to complete the restorations. Were the environments become unusable to researchers (e.g. due restoration works), most of the data would still

---

[8] Fichera *et al.* 2015 pp. 25-28.
[9] Osanna 2017.

[10] A third partner in the HCP, the British School at Rome, was involved until 2014. For more information, see: www.herculaneum.org
[11] Guidobaldi 2016.
[12] Laino *et al.* 2014.

be accessible digitally through the GIS system.[13]

When working on an ancient structure, one should consider that this has had a life of its own, an original function and, probably, several subsequent adaptations. The more complex a construction is, the more sophisticated was the technology adopted to build it. Therefore, a correct three-dimensional survey and a possible virtual reconstruction should take into account a considerable amount of information, including: previous surveys at different scales; digital and non-digital images; topographical data; historical data; context; construction techniques. In other words, it should be based on a philological process similar to the one originally implemented for the construction of the structure at hand[14].

Working in a 3D environment helps to neglect no component of the structure and to see everything in a homogeneous and coherent unit. Moreover, the virtual environment allows a reconstruction of the ancient environment and a contextual relocation, often indispensable to better understand technical construction choices or functions of particular areas.

The 3D model can be modified, integrated and constantly updated, and information can be extracted at any time. Any photorealistic texture becomes a fundamental support for the maintenance and conservation of the asset, and also the basis to reconstruct the original state. This reconstruction, if operated with the constant support of specialists, becomes a powerful tool for enhancement and to facilitate the users.

4.2 Pompeii, Domus of Eros Stallius (I,6,13-14)

As part of the 3D-ICONS project, aimed at the digitisation of architectural and archaeological masterpieces of European culture,[15] several large three-dimensional surveys were acquired in Pompeii by CISA (Centro Interdipartimentale Servizi di Archeologia) of the University of Naples "L'Orientale"[16]. The work was focused on less known archaeological areas, but still highly relevant for the analysis of the building techniques and the stratigraphic super-impositions that occurred over time.

One of these areas is the domus known as the *Domus of Eros Stallius* (Regio I, Insula 6, 13-14) (Figure 39). This *domus*, although neglected by recent archaeological research, preserves a rich vertical stratigraphy that covers a wide chronological period and offers interesting information on the development of this side of the ancient city (Figure 40).

A complex site such as the one of Pompeii, which consists of a wide range of structural types with different levels of

detail, inevitably requires the use of more techniques and 3D survey methods.

The *domus* was brought to light between 1926 and 1927, by the archaeologist Amedeo Maiuri[17], but no precise stratigraphic data have been recorded and studied. It had two levels currently evidenced by two stairways. It was relatively small by Roman standards, with about 300 sqm. for the first floor. The rooms were exposed on the western side of the *atrium tuscanicum*, while the access to a small garden was on the northern side. This area (*tablinum*) had an *opus signinum* floor ('cocciopesto') decorated with white tiles with a pattern of meanders and rhombus. A complex hydraulic system was built before the house was destroyed. The renovation work was certainly carried out a few years before the eruption of 79 AD. Some coins found during the excavation suggest a date around 65 AD.

According to Maiuri's hypothesis, the house was completely in ruins even before the eruption of Vesuvius. He concluded that the large pile of sand found in the rooms around the *atrium* made this house unusable and also indicated that the rooms had probably been adapted as private storage for building materials. In his excavation report, Maiuri shows a photo taken at the moment of excavation where it is clearly visible, under the pumice stone (the white layer in the photo) of the eruption, a dark deposit suggesting the poor state of the house already before 79 AD.

As part of the project *Pompeian Households: An Online Companion*, professor Penelope M. Allison has included this house in a group of 30 so-called "atrium houses". All, except one, have at least one garden in addition to the atrium.

After the excavation in the 1920s, no in-depth analysis has been carried out in this area. Between 2014 and 2015, the study of this house is resumed as part of a master's thesis at the University of Naples "L'Orientale".

The research project was developed when the GPP Knowledge Plan was starting – this focused on the correct use of innovative investigation techniques.

To preserve these types of historical monuments the right interpretation of the different construction phases is crucial. For example, in this case, the simple observation of the walls of the house allows to notice the different heterogeneous structural interventions occurred over time. Many architectural techniques are recognizable, among the oldest known in the city (i.e. light frame constructions) alternating with more modern techniques.

One of the objectives of the intervention was to create a complete 3D model capable of replacing the traditional record of archaeological documentation of structures,

---

[13] Court *et al.* 2011
[14] Amici 2008
[15] See also paragraph 1.3.
[16] Bosco et al. 2015; Bosco et al. 2016

[17] Maiuri 1929

Figure 39. Aerial image of the Domus of Eros Stallius.

Figure 40. General plan of Pompeii. In the red area the Domus of Stallius Eros.

unifying geometric information with structural information.

In June 2014, the team of the University of Naples "L'Orientale", under the supervision of Prof. Fabrizio Pesando, started the cleaning of the *domus* with the aim of carrying out a detailed examination of the house and reconstructing its original structure. During this intervention numerous investigations were carried out to provide a complete 3D model of the house. Different methodologies and technologies were used and the final results were compared to measure their precision, effectiveness and speed. At the beginning, the *domus* was analysed by means of an electronic total station, commonly used for the archaeological survey. Then two other interventions were designed, with close-range photogrammetry, to output a 3D replica of the house.

The survey was of particular interest also because, just after this survey campaign, the site was closed for technical reasons. Therefore, the study of the site could continue thanks to the data recorded also through these 3D models.

The 'total station' is a device commonly used survey in o perform for 'indirect' archaeological surveys. This methodology has become quite cheap and the management software is particularly user-friendly, even for unskilled operators. The survey of the Eros Stallius *domus* included the acquisition of points necessary to build a general plan of the house with the addition of a few selected points for recording the heights and some irregular floors. Figure 41 shows the results of the survey after processing the data obtained with the total station using CAD software.

This type of operation required a full day on site for two archaeologists appointed to align and recalibrate the instrument to acquire the points defining the dimensions of walls, holes and water canalization of the *domus* and the average heights and depths.

The total station captured in detail the characteristics of the vertical stratigraphy of the walls of the house. Nevertheless, it would take a long time of acquisition with an inevitable approximation of the smallest details.

To overcome this limitation of the total station, two different photogrammetric surveys were performed.

47

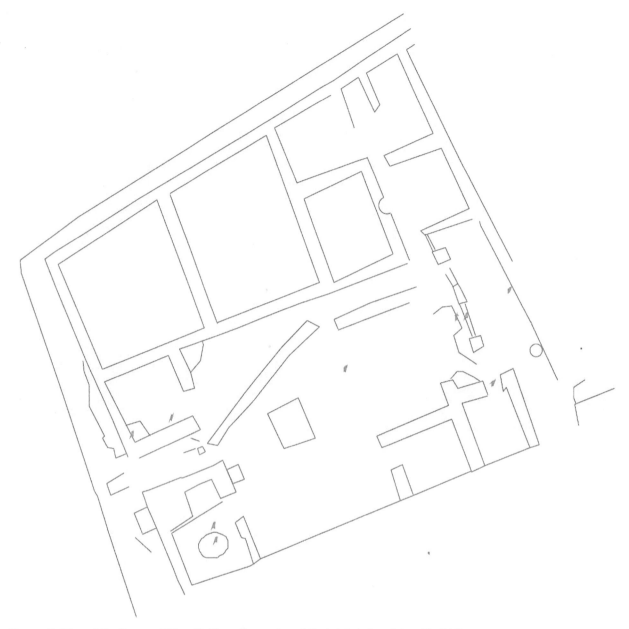

Figure 41. Plan of the *Domus* of *Eros Stallius* – Processing of the total station data with CAD.

The first was performed with a terrestrial technique. About 1,500 photos were taken with a Nikon D90 reflex camera to cover the entire *domus*. Previously some targets were placed on the walls and measured with the total station, to define the geometry of the archaeological structure and align the final model to the 'traditional' survey. The on-site acquisition took only a few hours and required the work of two archaeologists using a topographic pole for the camera and a ladder to acquire the highest parts of the structure in a homogeneous way.

A second intervention was carried out with a low-cost drone (Apollo IdeaFly) equipped with a small compact digital camera (Canon PowerShot SX 260) and making use of the continuous shooting function. To gain flying time and consequently increase the number of shots, the drone was lightened and the equipment reduced. Moreover, the camera was fixed directly to the drum of the

drone in a perpendicular position by using a lightweight mount to reduce the vibration of the drone, since this was not equipped with the appropriate gimbal. Also for the aerial intervention some targets were positioned and acquired with total station to ensure the accurate scaling of the model and a successful overlap of the different reliefs.

The use of terrestrial and aerial shots was necessary to integrate the two different perspectives from a lower and a higher point of view. For the acquisition of the upper part of the walls ladders and rods were used, while the roofs and the upper part of the walls were acquired with the drone.

Since the area is accessible to tourists, the team was forced to schedule the flight before the archaeological site was open to the public, i.e. in the early hours of the morning, when light conditions are not optimal. To mitigate the poor

Figure 42. Image of the terrestrial photogrammetric survey of the *domus* of Eros Stallius with the positioning of the shots (in blue).

light conditions, the team set the ISO value to 400, to get visibility without causing excessive noise on the photos. The shutter speed was set to its maximum, i.e. 1/2000 – the movements of the drone and the continuous shooting allowed to take more shots than it was necessary.

This redundancy of photos allowed selecting high quality photos in the pre-processing phase, without losing the necessary overlap. The results obtained were very satisfactory (Figure 43), considering that it was neither possible to set a route before the flight nor to know the height reached by the drone. During the 8 minutes of flight, several hundred photos were acquired from an estimated height of about 15 meters.

The data processing was performed by using the photogrammetry software Agisoft Photoscan while for a better post-production of the mesh (surface) Geomagic Studio® and MeshLab software were used.

Figure 43. View from the top of the domus survey obtained by aerial photogrammetric acquisition.

Despite the different, unconventional adjustments applied to the drone, the result of the flight was satisfactory. The photos, after a necessary careful selection (about 200 photos were actually used), presented a very good overlap. Moreover, high resolution allowed to create a model of about 21,600,000 faces.

On the other hand, the quality of the photos from the ground was much higher. Despite the high resolution and the large number of shots (and therefore also the high 'weight' of the whole project) we decided to process all the photos in a single batch. The dense cloud obtained with an average processing was about 98,000,000 points and the mesh relief included more than 225,000,000 faces. (Figure 44)

A 3D survey with these features is almost impossible to manage, even on a high-power machine. Therefore, it was decided to apply some simplifications to obtain a model with about one tenth of the initial information. This final model was chosen after an accurate comparison of different versions, by balancing the model's manageability and the level of accuracy required for the survey purposes.

Nevertheless, due to the high resolution the texturization required a temporary disassembly of the survey in 4 parts. Each part was individually textured and saved. The survey was then, very easily, thanks to some georeferencing, recomposed within by using the Geomagic software.

To compare the two photogrammetric models, a very interesting wall was chosen for the analysis of the development of the house which presents one of the oldest construction techniques used in Pompeii, the *opera a telaio* (i.e. light frame construction). This wall (the east wall of the atrium) is 6.25 m long, according to the reading obtained from the total station, while the same surface is 6.28 m in the model derived from terrestrial photogrammetry. The errors with the use of the total station are generally due to the calibration of the instrument and the manual inaccuracy in the positioning of the targets needed to record the exact position of the points to be acquired. This error is generally less than 0.5% of the total length (that is less than 3 cm on 6.25 m). For this reason, the technique provides very reliable measurements for linear walls and is therefore considered reliable for archaeological surveys at average distance. Moreover, the difference between the measurements obtained from the total station and the one obtained from the uncalibrated terrestrial photogrammetry is about 3 cm (respectively 6.25 vs 6.28). Therefore, the two techniques seem to have the comparable reliability.

The primary objective of the surveys was providing detailed and accurate support for archaeological research, with low-cost intervention and by considering management problems that often involve three-dimensional investigation. The use and integration of the results obtained from the use of the three methodologies allowed to identify the trade-offs of each technique.

Figure 44. Image of the 3D replica obtained via terrestrial photogrammetry.

The use of the total station to obtain digital plans is currently routine on archaeological excavations. Traditionally, this activity is simplified, as archaeologists only need to know the size of the construction and its location. Additional details are commonly assigned to cards, photos, sections, etc. . . .

By acquiring a three-dimensional survey all this information can be easily extracted from the reconstruction. Consistently with this it has been possible, through the cutting of virtual planes, to obtain maps and sections to a level of detail that allowed an easy analysis of the deterioration of the walls (Figure 45).

Since orthophotos and ortho-rectified maps can easily be extracted from the from the 3D model[18] the archaeologist can have at any time a precise and measurable digital resource 1:1 scale. This will allow the identification of building techniques and masonry stratigraphy. This is because orthophotos and ortho-rectified are characterized by a detailed and colourful description of the surface. During the processing phase, the technique also removes any modern detail that hinders a complete reading and interpretation of the archaeological feature. In this *domus*, an overall frontal view of the western outer wall was impossible because it is situated on a very narrow road. A normal straightened mosaic photo would certainly have created distortions. The high detail obtained with the photogrammetric relief from the ground provided high-resolution, metric and distortion-free (even chromatic) orthophoto-photo (Figure 46).

Low-cost aerial photogrammetry did not provide enough detail to extract specific information, but it was useful for planimetric analysis and context view (the roof, the upper part of the high walls and the narrow streets surrounding the house).

Data was acquired by cameras with different resolutions at different times. Therefore, the final models have different properties. The integration of the two reconstructions, a complete view of the context with the drone survey and a detailed interior with the ground survey, provided several useful information for the archaeological interpretation of the house[19]. We used the open source CloudCompare software to obtain an adequate comparison (from the metric point of view) of the two 3D measurements obtained. [20] This software processes point clouds and triangular meshes. CloudCompare was created to compare point clouds from laser scanner surveys. It has been then implemented in a point cloud processing software to perform many elaborations on them. We inserted two dense point clouds into the program and superimposed. A cloud-cloud distance analysis was then performed using the Hausdorff distance algorithm. This algorithm, which is based on the analysis of how two subsets of a metric space

are arranged together, simply takes into account the closest minimum distance. Figure 47 shows the overlapping of the two models. For a better understanding, four classes have been chosen to identify the variations. The overlap shows a good alignment: the distance between the two models is less than 5 cm in 72% (blue and green). The variance in yellow, ranging from 5 to 7.5 cm (14.2%), seems to locate mainly along the vertical lines of the highest wall where the drone probably failed to capture the surfaces correctly. Finally, the high percentage (about 13.3%) of deviations greater than 7.5 cm (in red) seems to coincide with parts that have completely disappeared in the model (e.g. the crests of the walls) or areas that have changed a lot in the time elapsed between the two surveys (e.g. at the time of the aerial data acquisition the *tablinum* had been reburied, therefore it was not visible).

To better understand the presence of areas of great difference between terrestrial and aerial investigation, a precise analysis was carried out by examining the highest wall in the eastern part of the house adjacent to *Domus* I, 6, 15.

Applying the same analysis on this part of the model the results are very different (Figure 48). 40% shows a good overlap while 60% shows a distance greater than 5 cm. This large discrepancy is due to the surface of the wall being captured by the drone camera which can only shoot in a vertical position. Moreover, since the acquisition of the drone was carried out in the early morning hours, before the opening of the archaeological area, for safety reasons, the wall, which was particularly high, was still very shaded at the time of the flight (Figure 43).

Probably, with more sunlight, the overlap would have been better. This is clear when comparing individual walls (Figure 49). In the first image the surface of the wall is poorly defined, with many incomplete areas compared to the model obtained from the terrestrial survey. On the latter model the whole wall is complete and well represented.

The absence of stratigraphic information makes the correct reading of the vertical stratigraphy paramount. This is the only source of information on changes in the house (extension possibility, reduction, difference in alignments). The traditional approach – of the archaeological study of masonry structures – foresees cataloguing with photos that have metric reference. Sometimes these photos are adjusted. Orthophotos are very rare. In the case of *Eros Stallius*, the three-dimensional metrically valid copy of the structure was fundamental to continue the investigation when the domus was banned to the public.

Moreover, the integration of different techniques is particularly useful for the survey of high structures. This integration not only solves visibility problems (e.g. a niche cannot be seen from above; an inaccessible roof cannot be captured by terrestrial photogrammetry; etc), but could improve the definition and measurement of vertical and horizontal planes of the walls to reduce any distortion.

[18] Bornaz *et al.* 2006.
[19] D'Andrea, Barbarino 2012.
[20] http://www.danielgm.net/cc/

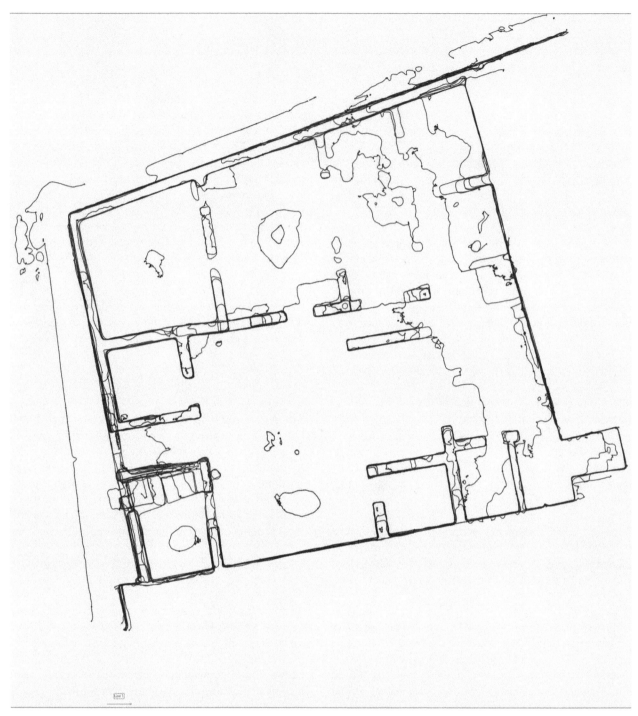

Figure 45. Planimetry obtained from the automatic extraction of contour lines on the three-dimensional relief.

Figure 46. Orthophoto of the external west wall of the *Domus* di Eros Stallius from terrestrial photogrammetric survey.

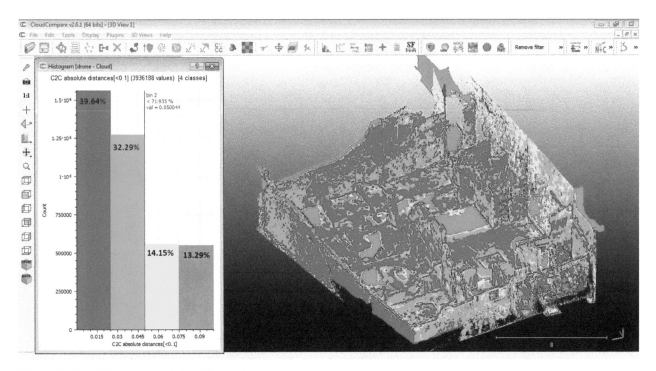

Figure 47. CloudCompare analysis of dense clouds.

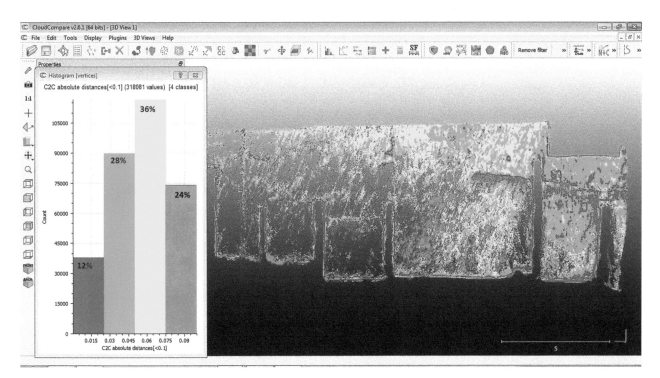

Figure 48. CloudCompare analysis of the sections of dense cloud on the wall and *domus*.

4.3 Pompei, Domus del Centauro (VI,9,3)

In the framework of the project *Living in Pompeii in the Samnite Age: 3D digital documentation of the pre-Roman dwellings of Regio VI in Pompeii*, a three-dimensional survey was carried out involving the *Domus del Centauro* (VI, 9, 3-5) (Figure 50). This project was managed at the Centro Interdipartimentale di Servizi di Archeologia (CISA) of the University of Naples "L'Orientale". The *domus*, which overlooks Via di Mercurio, is among those involved in the 'Regio VI project'. The project involved the Universities of Naples L'Orientale, Venice, Siena and Trieste, and systematically studied the Domus *insulae* between years 2000 and 2010. The archaeological investigations carried out in this house identified the so-called *Protocasa del Centauro* (VI,9,3) (Figure 51), dating back to the second half of the 3rd century B.C. This house has a peculiar architectural structure that has given back some important information on the decorative apparatus of the middle Samnite age (Such as the mosaic of the

Figure 49. Dense points cloud of the wall from aerial shooting (left) and terrestrial shooting (right).

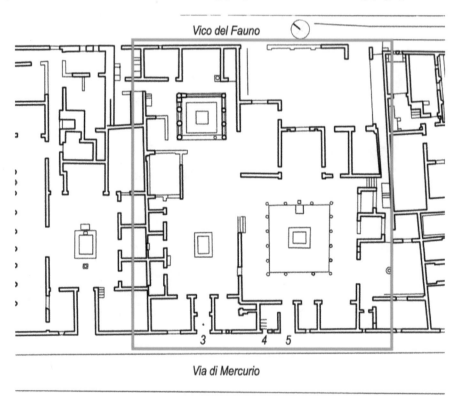

Figure 50. Plan of the late Republican phase of the *Domus del Centauro*.

tablinum with a *cocciopesto* with a threshold decorated in regular puncta and a tessellated pattern framed in red and white bands, among the oldest attested in the Magna Graecia and Siceliote area)[21].

The structure of the proto-house has been well preserved thanks to the enormous filling (about 60 cm.) that raised the floor to radically reorganize the houses during the second half of the II century B.C. The materials found in the massive filling were fundamental to confirm the period of use of the proto-house (about a century). The structure of the archaic house was investigated with stratigraphic

---

[21] Pesando 2009

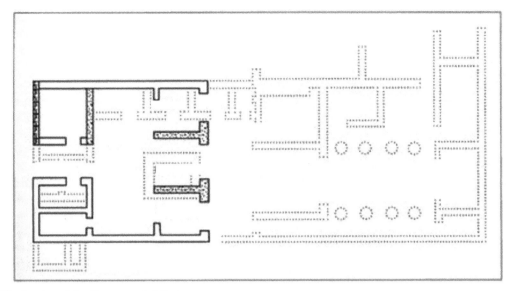

Figure 51. Planimetry of the *Protocasa del Centauro*.

excavations, except for the part under the cubicle with alcove that did not require so, given the good state of conservation of the flooring (Figure 52). In this case, non-invasive methods such as geoelectric resonance were used.

The structure of the *Proto-casa del Centauro* is not immediately comparable to any of the housing types known for Pompeii. It does not fall within the typology of the *Atrio Tuscanico* houses, nor within the so called "terraced houses" typical of the regions I and II. However, comparisons within Pompeii are still relevant (for example, it finds great similarities with entrance 3 of the House of *Julius Polibius*). Given the exceptionality and, therefore, the importance, from a scientific point of view, of the domus, it was decided to deepen the documentation with the acquisition of a 3D survey that used the image-based photogrammetry technique – Structure from Motion (SfM) (Figure 53).

This allowed to combine an accurate metric survey to high quality photographic resolution being able to reinterpret the masonry layers. This methodology was chosen mainly for the photorealistic restitution of the three-dimensional data, but also for the expeditious acquisition of useful data to the survey (essentially photographic shots) and integrability with the metric data acquired with total station or GPS, inserted as GCPs – Ground Control Points. This combination allowed for scaling and optimizing the 3D model. For the complete acquisition of the *domus* area coinciding with the *Protocasa del Centauro*, 2220 photographs were taken with a Nikon D90 SLR camera with 18 mm lens (Figure 54). The acquisition presented many difficulties, because the environments varied from wide and very illuminated open spaces to narrow and dark areas (such as the Cubicle with alcove). Other difficulties were caused by the high columns of the pseudo *peristilio* behind the tablinum and the difference in height of the walls of the rooms (strongly damaged by the bombardments of World War II).

Therefore, the work required a scrupulous planning of the on-site acquisition, assisted by telescopic supports for high heights, to cover all surfaces.

The control points acquisition was performed with a Trimble Total Station after the photographic acquisition (Figure 56). The topographic survey was carried out by hooking into the topographic network of Pompeii, of which cornerstones and their monographs are known. Moreover, new temporary stations were located inside the Domus, to acquire the widest view.

To ensure adequate coverage and proper optimization of the model numerous points have been acquired within the *domus* (Figure 55).

The points were chosen overlooking the elevations or in non-movable elements on the ground that may be easily recognized and individualized on a photo during post production within the software (Figure 57).

Figure 52. Detail of the floor in the Alcove Cubicle

Figure 53. Photographic and topographical field acquisition operations in order to obtain the photogrammetric survey of the *Domus*.

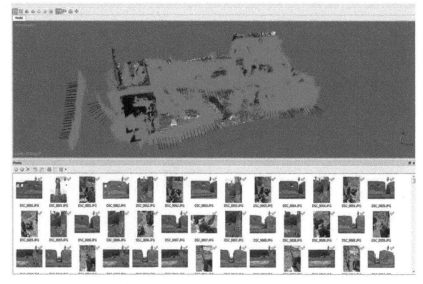

Figure 54. Location of the shots (in blue) on the 3D cloud.

To ensure an accurate base and replace photogrammetry points in the most difficult areas (e.g. columns or areas with a lot of vegetation), 4 laser scans were acquired with the FARO FOCUS 3D X130 laser scanner tool (Figure 58). Due to the linear trend of the *domus*, three scans were enough for the extraction of the remaining control points.

During the processing with Agisoft Photoscan software we divided the project into two chunks, for different zones. This was done due to the large number of shots and the extreme difference in the parameters set for each acquisition. Indeed, the differences could confuse the software and affect successful alignment. Therefore, one

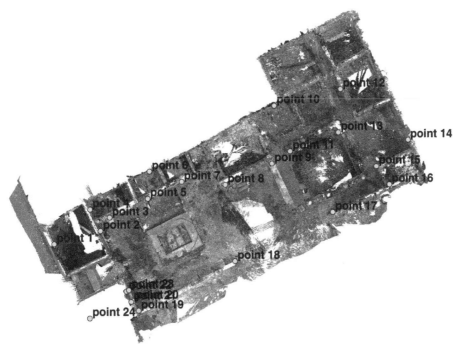

Figure 55. Visualization on the cloud of the topographic control points acquired with the Total Station.

Figure 56. Total Station located in the *domus atrium*.

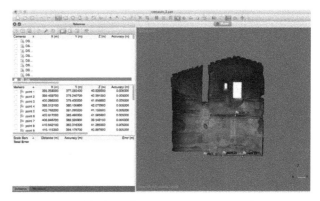

Figure 57. Positioning of some points on a wall of the 3D replica (West wall of the cubicle with Alcove).

chunk was dedicated to the single covered room with best preserved wall decoration, namely the Alcove Cubicle and its well-known magnificent example of first style. The second chunk was dedicated to all the remaining spaces of the Domus. The processing of 'model 1' generated a scattered point cloud of about 220,000 points and a dense cloud of about 134 million points (Figure 59). The cubicle model alone generated a scattered cloud of about 135,000 points and a dense cloud of about 22 million points. Such a dense cloud allows us to appreciate, already at this stage, the 3D survey quality detail (Figure 60 and Figure 61).

The two dense clouds were then joined in one cloud without gaps through the common control points. Finally, we created the meshes, i.e. polygon surfaces on which the same images acquired and used for the creation of the 3D model were applied to obtain high-resolution ortho-photomosaics of walls and floors (Figure 62). Hence, it is always possible to produce a processing report, containing information on the camera settings, the photographs, the overlap between

Figure 58. Visualization in CAD environment of the point cloud obtained by laser scanning.

them, the number of homologous points, the control points and their average error. Therefore, it is possible to obtain a model of the walls (DEM) (Figure 63) for a quick and immediate visualization of the metric data, and to extract level curves that can be exported in a CAD environment.

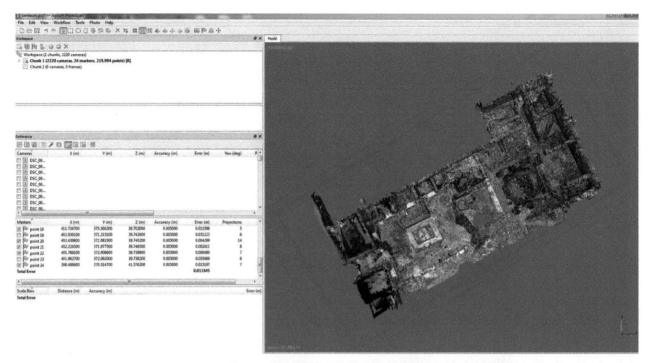

Figure 59. Dense point cloud of the domus. Top view in Agisoft Photoscan software.

Figure 60. Detail of the dense coloured cloud of the Cubicle with Alcove.

Figure 61. Dense cloud uncoloured. Detail of the Domus *atrium.*

Figure 62. Ortho-photo of the west wall of the *Cubicle with Alcove.*

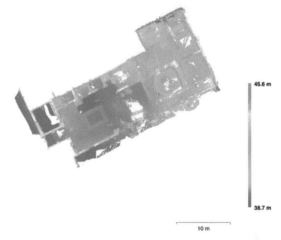

Figure 63. Digital elevation model (DEM) of *Domus del Centauro.*

From the three-dimensional model it is possible to extract information at any time (plants and sections at the desired heights, orthophotos, heights, etc. . .).

The model creation process is always repeatable to obtain models with different resolution (for example less detailed and, therefore, lighter model for educational purposes, or more detail one for single rooms or walls.

Moreover, due to the high accuracy of the 3D survey, it is possible to easily monitor the state of the structures by repeating the acquisitions over time. Indeed, by inserting the same GCPs (Ground Control Points), a direct comparison of the models obtained at different times is possible – this allows to identify any misalignment or failure.

Finally, the orthophotos extracted from the 3D model are correct in all their levels, unlike common photo-rectifications. Therefore, niches, windows and *lararia* are metrically valid and measurable. The photos obtained in this way can provide support for analyses of structural or decorative degradation of the walls. Moreover, the photos can integrate the archaeological files (USM).

5

Building Information Modelling for Cultural Heritage

The Historic Building Information Modelling (HBIM) 'is a novel library of prototype parametric objects, based on historic architectural data and a system of cross platform systems to map the parametric objects onto point cloud and image survey data'[1].

The HBIM system is often associated to reverse engineering on existing buildings, as it analyses the construction processes that generated them. This process is synthetised in a database which is aimed at *ad hoc* maintenance and management of the asset[2], on the basis of the three-dimensional model.

During the modelling it is therefore necessary to recreate parametric objects that represent a digital replica of the elements that compose the existing historical architecture.

Some studies have addressed the issue of creating standard libraries of architectural elements from point clouds, but they mainly refer to classical architecture[3]. The construction of specific parametric objects applicable to historical architecture cannot disregard their semantic value. Only in this way can they potentially be used in all models of existing buildings with similar characteristics.

The definition of a three-dimensional model of a historical heritage is strictly connected to the evaluation of the reliability and adherence to reality of the model itself; the question of the *level of reliability* (LOR), represents the latest and most up-to-date point of arrival in the discussion about the use of digital models of cultural heritage.

Reliability of a digital product involves various aspects, including the systematic collection of any previous archival documentation, the recording of the reports of each phase of digital data acquisition, the setting of the equipment and the characteristics of the point cloud, and the sharing of the information processing phases[4]. In applications, the efforts to codify and measure the LOR in relation to a BIM output applied to Cultural Heritage have focused on the issues of geometric and volumetric accuracy of the asset components. Unfortunately, less attention has been paid for the scientific reliability of the informative and semantic contents that complete a BIM database.

Many scientific papers in the field of HBIM tend to 'simplify' the construction of objects, starting from sections of point clouds or orthophotos extracted from the model. In the built heritage the architectural elements are often well preserved[5] and the creation of categories of objects is quite simple. On the other hand, in the archaeological context the structures are very often badly preserved and only partially visible or strongly restored and, in some cases, modified with respect to their original form. In these cases, there are no shared libraries of elements with corresponding descriptions and this makes data management more difficult. For these reasons, few models have so far been tested in the archaeological field[6].

The creation of a 3D model is considered an essential element in the planning of a BIM system of the historical building; the acquisition of the point cloud represents the first stage of a process that, from the metric survey, aims at the creation of a parametric model, which also provides formal, structural and compositional information (Figure 64). Then, there is the geometric definition through 2D drawings of the elements that are not complete or completely measurable within the point cloud, to facilitate and speed up the modelling activities.

Note that some complex architectural elements and, particularly, the decorative elements in the built heritage are modelled from scratch, as they are unique objects that are not included in the system families of the software. Therefore, recent research is investing in algorithms for classifying point clouds and 3D surfaces in an attempt to simplify the process of modelling complex objects. Unfortunately, to date, we are still far from a rapid and linear process that can easily define the practice of "scans to BIM" for Cultural Heritage.

The creation of a BIM for Cultural Heritage allows an in-depth investigation on the asset, since it needs the assessment of position, function, geometry, composition and state of conservation of each component.

5.1 ABIM

With the term ArcheoBIM (ABIM) scholars[7] wanted to distinguish archaeological cases from cultural heritage in general, because of their peculiar, and often unique, characteristics. In fact, compared to the historical building, the archaeological structures often have as their only reference the information coming from the excavation. There are very few cases (e.g. Vitruvius) in which specific

[1] Murphy 2012
[2] Saygi, Remondino 2013
[3] For more information see recent revisions Lopez *et al.* 2018 end Carpentiero 2018.
[4] Bianchini, Nicastro 2018

[5] Quattrini *et al.* 2015
[6] Scianna *et al.* 2015
[7] Garagnani *et al.* 2016; Bosco et al. 2018; Bosco et al. 2020; Garagnani et al. 2021

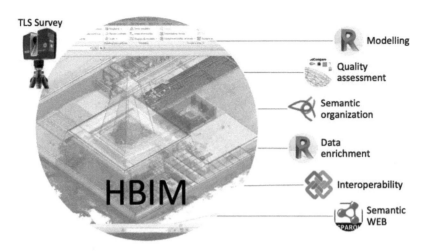

Figure 64. HBIM procedure.

written sources on the technologies used by ancient builders have come down to us[8]. To apply BIM methodologies in archaeology means, therefore, to operate a process of reverse engineering, that starting from the real object, or from the traces of it, builds a digital parametric version of it. This parametric system becomes an interactive and interoperable container of archaeological, 3D geometric and environmental information, thanks to a performing database interface of the dedicate software.

For both HBIM and ABIM, the Information System is fundamental, which is the elaborated set of information that can be loaded inside the BIM model and referred to each parametric object (Figure 65). In both declinations of BIM applied to cultural heritage, the collection of information related to the object, or to the examined context, is a fundamental phase, preparatory to the creation of the digital model itself.

Once the semantic structure that serves as the basis for the ABIM model has been established, the next steps are the collection of structural data relating to the materials used within the context and the definition of construction techniques. Once this stage is completed, it is possible to start a critical reading of the set of information available and, consequently, to establish the specifications of the parametric modelling. It will then be possible to organise thematic libraries of families of objects and libraries of materials connected to these families, based on the construction techniques identified within the context.

It is clear that the process of creating historical libraries is not simple and requires great care. In a library for Cultural Heritage, the families of objects cannot contain rigid schemes; on the contrary, they must be editable by the user, in order to guarantee respect for the form and uniqueness of the elements represented[9].

The geometric accuracy of the three-dimensional data in a BIM system is a fundamental requirement for the good functioning of the whole process; the structural analyses, calculations and reconstructive hypotheses that are speed up with a BIM model, necessarily pass through the geometric correctness of the three-dimensional data they manage. Therefore, including a phase of validation of the quality of the metric base used in an ABIM project, as happens in engineering projects, is of paramount importance.

Once all the information data are obtained and the semantic library is built, it is possible obtaining the virtual reconstruction of the asset.

Thanks to the properties of BIM, is possible a proper reconstruction of partially preserved structures or a queryable representation of the building in its different construction/chronological phases.

5.2 The Solar Temple of Nuserra (Abu Gurab – Egypt)

In 2010, more than one hundred years after the discovery by the German archaeologist Ludwig Borchardt[10], an Italian mission resumed the investigations at the Solar Temple of Niuserra in Abu Ghurab. The site is located about 15 km south of Cairo, in Egypt. Professor Rosanna Pirelli, Dr. Andrea D'Andrea (University of Naples "L'Orientale") and Dr. Massimiliano Nuzzolo (Oriental and Mediterranean Cultures, Varsavia) supervised the research.

The research is mainly intended to reassess, at a high level, the archaeological data still available on site in order to establish an updated plan of the temple by using new technologies[11].

---

[8] Garagnani 2017

[9] Achille *et al.* 2014

[10] The investigations are resumed thanks to the study: Nuzzolo 2010 "The Solar Temples and the Royal Ideology in the Old Kingdom". (Ph.D. dissertation, University of Naples "L'Orientale")

[11] Bosco et al. 2018; Bosco et al. 2019; Nuzzolo et al. 2020

Figure 65. Visualisation of the information sheet containing basic data of a wall entity. Insula 4-6 of Paestum, graphic elaboration by Laura Carpentiero.

The objective of the digital investigation was the virtual reconstruction of the monument to verify the compatibility of the structural hypothesis formulated by Borchardt at the beginning of the last century. Since several parts of the temple were partially damaged, due to the continuous reuse of the stones of the walls, it was essential to locate exactly the position of each block or wall. The temple of the sun shows a large sample of blocks and architectural elements whose analysis is of paramount importance to reconstruct the missing parts of the monument.

The digital survey, performed by laser scanner and image-based modelling technique, is the first real 3D replica of the temple.

In four acquisition campaigns[12] numerous surveys were carried out using different devices, with the aim of reconstructing the overall archaeological area of the temple of Niuserra.

As mentioned just above, the building showed many gaps and missing parts. For this reason, the design of the data acquisition was particularly accurate in order to avoid errors in the reconstruction.

The first fundamental step was the implementation of a local topographic grid to ensure support for translation and alignment of the scans.

In 2010 the surveys focused on the area of the Chapel and the so-called Seasons Room in the southern part of the temple, as well as the warehouse area in the north-eastern part of the temple[13], the obelisk and altar area[14].

At the end of the missions the total number of scans acquired with the Zoller & Froilich 5003 laser scanner, were 47. All scans were processed, recorded and aligned based on the points measured by the total station.

Since the laser scanner used for the above-mentioned surveys is not able to acquire colour data, some photos were taken with a digital camera and superimposed to the final 3D to obtain a more realistic model. The process was semi-manual, (i.e. consisted in identifying a sufficient number of homologous points between the 3D model and the photo to obtain a texture).

The surveys were fundamental to obtain a large amount of information on the state of the monument. From a top view of the model it was possible to generate a plan showing the perimeter of the obelisk, the inner corridor and the collapse of the walls in the south-west corner. The plan was then elaborated characterizing the blocks used for the outer and inner side of the obelisk. Finally, the plan was superimposed on the original map, drawn up by Borchardt after the discovery, in order to compare the reconstruction obtained from the model so obtained with the survey carried out by the German archaeologist (Figure 66).

---

[12] Two campaigns were carried out in 2010, another one in December 2014 and a final one in 2017. I was involved in the last two missions as a member of the research team, for acquisition and 3D restitution. Among others, the following researchers participated to the mission: Giancarlo Iannone (ZF laser scanner acquisition), Emanuele Brienza (Topography), Patrizia Zanfagna (Survey and restitution).

[13] January 2010 mission.
[14] December 2010 mission.

In 2011, due to a political change in the country, parts of the court floor and the masonry of the obelisk were partially damaged, including two areas:

1. the Seasons Room, presented damages to the floor;
2. the large staircase of the so-called storages, in the northeast corner, were completely destroyed.

Damages to the latter resulted in the loss of valuable information about this type of structure, whose presence is very rare in other contemporary royal complexes.

Moreover, the topographic grid (cemented metal pegs) had been completely removed.

In 2014, an on-site mission was rescheduled to continue the survey and to document the state of the structures.

This time a new type of laser scanner was available for the mission: the X130 3D Faro Focus (Figure 67). This instrument was mainly chosen because it offers the possibility to acquire original chromatic information by using an internal digital camera. These acquisitions are very useful to reconstruct not only the shape of the temple but also to understand the final texture of the temple itself and to provide a completely realistic 3D model of the sanctuary.

The new type of laser scanner can also acquire geo-referenced data, thanks to the integrated GPS. This option not only provides spatial information, but also allows faster and more precise automatic alignment of scans.

A further advantage offered by the new instrument is the lightness and, consequently, the manageability that allowed simplified the positioning inside the ruins.

During the mission we cover the entire temple area with the laser scanner. Particular attention was dedicated, however, to some specific areas, that were problematic for the final reconstruction of the monument or were important for the presence of numerous artefacts (that could be useful for the archaeological analysis of the temple and for a new planimetric analysis). In six days, 53 scans were acquired[15].

To achieve a more precise vision of the structure, we combined the laser scanner surveys with the Close-Range photogrammetry methodology. This better analysed and reconstructed the temple area and its architectural features.

Thus, we've acquired some critical areas with this technique, which were fundamental for the reconstruction of the obelisk and of the entire area:

---

[15] In detail: 10 scans for the low-resolution model of the Obelisk; 14 scans for the high-resolution model of the Obelisk; 10 scans for the main gate; 13 scans for the inner corridor of the obelisk; 6 scans for the walls closing the Sun Temple.

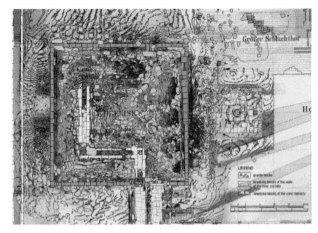

Figure 66. Image of the reconstructive model superimposed on the Borchardt planimetry (elaboration P. Zanfagna).

Figure 67. The Faro Focus 3D laser scanner survey: (a) a scanner in the interior corridor of the temple, (b) a scanner setting on the surrounding wall of the temple.

1. the main door of the temple;
2. the area of the so-called "Slaughterhouse" with the area of the alabaster basins;
3. the collapsing blocks located in the lower part of the obelisk in the south-west corner.

We obtained data with a Canon 450d DSLR of a 18mm lens and took us a day per area. We then processed the photos with Agisoft Photoscan software. We positioned some targets near the areas requiring investigation to be able to resize the model according to its real size. We extracted from the scans the coordinates of some points to verify the accuracy and precision of the work, and geo-reference the photogrammetric survey.

By examining the individual blocks, we have considered the following characteristics of design and construction of the temple:

- Simplicity: all the main elements of the architectural scheme of the building are easily visible. Through the recognition of the shape and colour of the materials, it

Figure 68. Survey of the basin area obtained with SfM technique.

is possible to associate each component to a system or subsystem in the overall architectural model;

- Modularity and standardization: they represent the uniformity of structural elements that are produced in series and with specific functions. These elements reduce the variability of components and facilitate the maintenance of individual elements throughout the temple;
- Portability: all architectural components of the main parts of the building are easily transportable and are characterized and installed as separate architectural units (or subsystems) that belong to the main system. In ancient times, this certainly facilitated the construction of the building but also the fast destruction and reuse of the material.

All these features are also visible in the contemporary pyramids of the nearby Abusir necropolis. Therefore, reliable comparisons can be performed to determine missing architectural elements.

Innovative research has been started from these architectural principles and considering the presence of partially destroyed elements, that analyses and compares different blocks and materials for the virtual reconstruction of the Temple of the Sun. All the available elements had to be taken into consideration to identify a main environmental and technological system and its subsystems.

To test a virtual reconstruction methodology, we adopted 'archaeological BIM' (ABIM) approach. It integrates the point clouds with the volumes and floors of the building. Thanks to BIM the concept of building design or modelling can be easily completed and enriched through a new and more complex environment. (Figure 69)

The experimentation, which began on the whole complex, was then limited to the area of the "Room of the Seasons". Scans and point clouds were imported into Autodesk's Recap software, cleaned and exported to have a single point cloud in a format (.rcp) that could be imported into Revit, Autodesk's BIM modelling software.

The first step of modelling focused on creating a conceptual mass that defines the levels to represent and contextualize the temple in its territory.

By assigning correct geographical coordinates it is possible to visualize the monument in its real landscape, with the aim of improving the final rendering according to the real positioning of the temple.

This global approach is particularly useful to generate correct shadows in animation and rendering, but also to deepen the spatial position of the monument. This is so as some temples have probably also been used as astronomical observation points. For this reason, the model was rotated according to the geographical north to ensure that the sunlight correctly illuminated all sides of the temple. The path of the sun was carefully simulated (Figure 70). In addition, the model was placed in an accurate topographical scenario based on surveys carried out during the campaigns or by extracting geographical data from existing cartography.

We have chosen different historical levels for the analysis. As also shown by Borchardt, the temple of Niuserra was located on a previous building whose traces are still partially visible in the ground. To identify the two monuments, we compared Borchardt's map with the data acquired from the digital survey.

First and second missions (2010)

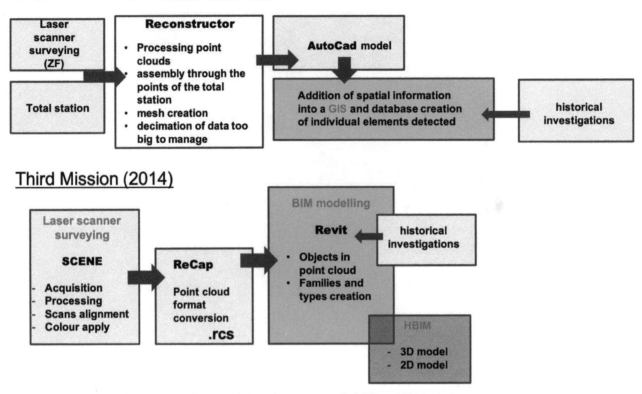

Third Mission (2014)

Figure 69. Workflow of data acquisition and elaboration processes in 2010 and 2014 missions.

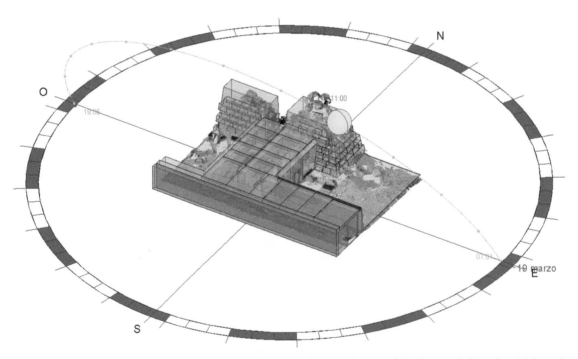

Figure 70. Simulation of the movement of the sun on the model, in Revit software, of the Seasonal Chamber (elaboration Patrizia Zanfagna).

We extracted from the analysis of the conceptual model some categories of architectural elements, corresponding to different components of the technological and construction system (Figure 71). These semantic parts contribute to the formal and physical representation of the 3D reconstruction of the monument. We have analysed and correctly assigned to a specific category each element of the subsystem.

Note that Revit software can create a taxonomy in the architectural model, including families, types and individual instances. Since Revit was designed primarily

TECHNOLOGICAL SYSTEM

classes of technological unit	technological units	classes of technical elements
Closing. Set of technological and technical elements of the building system with a function to separate and to conform the interior spaces of the building system itself than outside.		
	**vertical closure** set of vertical elements of the technical building system with a function to separate interior spaces of the building system itself than outside.	- perimeter walls - vertical external fixtures
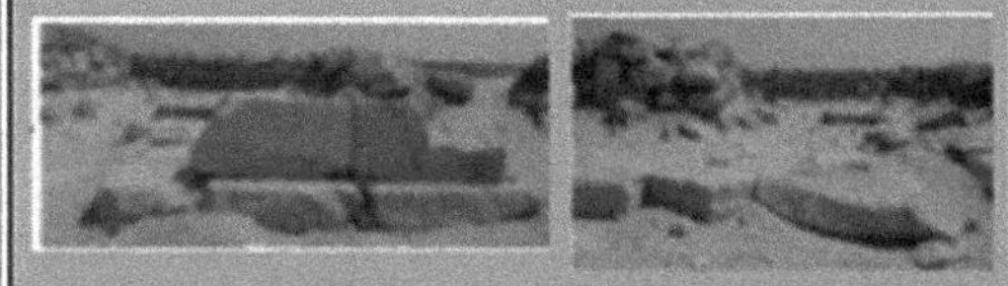	**lower horizontal closure** Set of horizontal technical elements of building system having function of separating the interior of the building system itself from the underlying soil or the foundation structures.	- Slab on the ground - horizontal fixtures
	**Horizontal closure of outdoor spaces** Set of horizontal technical elements of building system having function of separating the interior of the building system itself by underlying external spaces.	slabs of open spaces
	**top closure** Set of horizontal technical elements of building system having function of separating the interior of the building system itself from outer space above	- covers - horizontal external fixtures

Figure 71. Diagram of correlation between the parts of the temple and the technological classes

for industries and includes libraries or links to other specific libraries, the first step we took was implementing a new archive/library with a description of all archaeological artifacts.

Revit's conceptual design environment allows for analysing all components and creating classes or standard volumetric entities that can be integrated into the model.

These entities can be progressively converted into virtual building materials and, based on their volumetric families, we can create detailed architectural elements (walls, roofs, floors, etc.). Hence, the amount of building materials needed for the construction of each part or subsystem of the temple can be easily calculated. This also allow us to rapidly assess missing or destroyed elements.

Modelling tools (e.g. dynamic simulation of horizontal planes and virtual buildings) let us understand the original architectural structure of some of the temple components. This is extremely important for the obelisk, which shape and size has not yet been clarified and is one of the main objectives of investigation. For example, thanks to overlapping the cloud of points on the conceptual mass of the obelisk we were able to analyse the volumes of the

building to hypothesize dynamics of collapse in some areas or to move the blocks for the reconstruction of the monument (Figure 72).

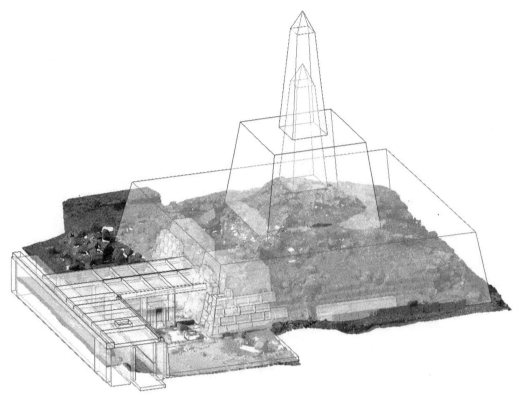

Figure 72. Overlapping of the two reconstructive models in BIM environment (Revit software elaboration P. Zanfagna).

6

Final Remarks

The archaeological documentation process can benefit from the introduction of sophisticated investigation techniques. These allow to significantly speed up many important operations an obtain accurate representations.

This publication presents some salient aspects of research undertaken in the context of 3D survey methods and *'integrated information management'*, for the purpose of studying the archaeological heritage, but also for its conservation and enhancement.

Survey technique in archaeology have always been the key tool for study and research, it has been shown that the advancement of new expeditious three-dimensional survey methodologies, and in particular the image-based ones (i.e. terrestrial photogrammetry and aerial) and range-based (i.e. laser scanner) in the field of cultural heritage, has led to the opening of new scenarios for developing the potential of the survey.

However, the cultural heritage research has devoted particular attention to the technical aspects related to the survey equipment. The research focused on issues such as of accuracy of the survey, its timing, ease of use and costs of the supports and of the data processing software. However, there is little research that deals with the systematic introduction of 3D investigations into the archaeological routine.

3D, on the one hand, has often been appreciated for its ability to provide a realistic representation of reality. On the other hand, its metric and analytical content has been underestimated. As a consequence, 3D has been particularly popular for dissemination purposes, but less appreciated in research contexts. Currently, archaeologists mainly use graphical representation through plans, sections and elevations for stratigraphic excavation, monuments and objects – such representation are the main tool the used to interpret and reconstruct the past. Such approach, however, reduces the three dimensions of reality into two-dimensions. This is based on some form of interpretation, and necessarily implies some loss of information, especially the volumetric data.

The management of digital information has been identified as one of the main issues about three-dimensional data for the archaeological heritage. Its management is made even more complex by the need for an integrated representation of various types of information in order to develop, for example, adequate archaeological conservation strategies. It does not simply end with the production of safe digital conservation standards, but requires a 'digital curation' activity, through which digital objects are managed over the entire life cycle – from creation and acquisition, to conservation, access and reuse.

Many researchers agree that scientific data cannot be correctly interpreted and reused with no information on how and in what circumstances the data was created (Provenance and Paradata). In the context of 3D digitalization, it is then crucial to define the range of technologies, tools and methodologies available for capturing and processing data. It is also essential to keep track of the different motivations and reasons behind any 3D digital replica – especially when sharing such findings. Making your data reusable is a key task to increase cooperation and collaboration between scientific research teams. For this purpose, metadata can be used to evaluate i) meaning, ii) relevance, iii) quality and iv) possibility of improvement and reworking.

The on-line 3D viewers (such as Sketcfab and 3DHOP) have made it possible to make the three-dimensional information accessible and navigable. These allow the user to carry out some useful operations such as taking measurements. On the other hand, they do not allow objective analysis of the survey and the digital object is 'filtered' on the basis of what its creator has chosen to communicate. Some recent research experiences (3D-ICONS) have made it possible to study solutions that allow the diffusion of 3D models in open libraries (Europeana), by attaching to these standard metadata schemes designed specifically for three-dimensional sources.

It has also been shown that the three-dimensional digital models of the existing archaeological heritage are essential representations for the management of heterogeneous data and should not be seen as a simple volumetric representation of an object. Conservation experts need to navigate documents, and perform multi-criteria queries in a virtual 3D environment to make any intervention decisions. For this purpose, the Archaeological Building Information Modelling (ABIM) or a digital representation of the physical and functional characteristics of an archaeological system is probably the most reliable shared resource of knowledge for the management of information over its life cycle.

The case study of the Niuserra Solar Temple in the Abu Gurab site shows that ABIM can be a convenient solution for the management and analysis of three-dimensional data within a multidisciplinary research process, following a linear methodological scheme as can be seen in the diagram in Figure 73.

ABIM facilitates the creation, in the architectural model, of a taxonomy including families, types and individual instances. This allows to analyse all the components and

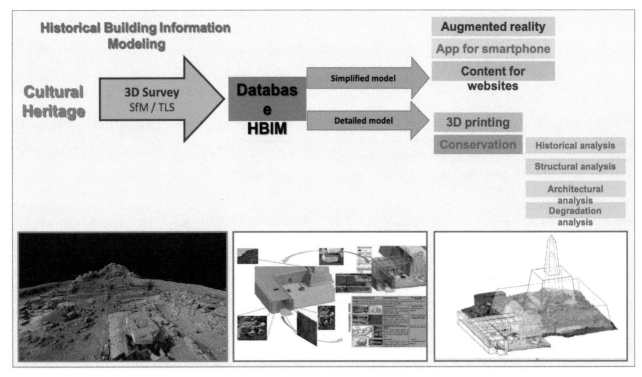

Figure 73. Scheme of applications of Building Information Modelling to cultural heritage implemented in the case study of the Solar Temple of Niuserra.

to create classes or single entities of standard volumes that can be integrated into the model.

Such entities can be progressively converted into virtual building materials. Based on their volumetric families, detailed architectural elements (walls, roofs, floors, etc.) can be created. This also allow to easily calculate the quantity of building materials necessary for the construction of each part or subsystem of the temple and to evaluate what is missing or has been destroyed.

Modelling tools, especially for the application of dynamic simulation of horizontal planes and virtual buildings, can also help to understand the original architectural structure of some of the components of the monument. This is extremely important for elements in which shape and size, as well as phenomena and dynamics of movement and possible collapse, are among the objectives of the investigation and are necessary for the final reconstruction of the monument.

Full use of such process requires a substantial investment by research in order to create specific libraries for the archaeological field.

Some direct research activities allowed to experiment the 3D documentation operations to satisfy the most common archaeological needs. In particular, the application to real cases representative of different research macro-topics such as study, conservation, and enhancement, allowed to:

• analyse the potential and critical issues of such innovative investigation methods;

• examine the difficulties of managing the data large scale date (big data) so obtained;

• investigate interoperability opportunities with archaeological activities such as excavation, conservation and enhancement.

These three phases were chosen since representing the pillars of a process of knowledge and safeguarding of the archaeological heritage. These can be carried out independently but present some contingencies.

For each of them, two case studies have been selected and studied in order to deal with the aspects of the three-dimensional restitution of data through specific interpretations. This was to contribute to the definition of an integrated methodological approach. (Figure 74).

6.1 Survey for excavation documentation

When discussing the case studies of San Biagio alla Venella and the Ancient Appia Landscapes, we deal, at a very high level, with the issue of survey for excavation documentation. In both cases, indeed, the stratigraphic investigation process is part a more extended territorial analysis.

The case study of the sanctuary of S. Biagio in the Metaponto area presents the typical problems of research that was resumed after a long time. Partial documentation, from non-digital media and at different scales, often makes integration with new data and planning of interventions difficult. A thorough comprehension of the environmental context can also be challenging.

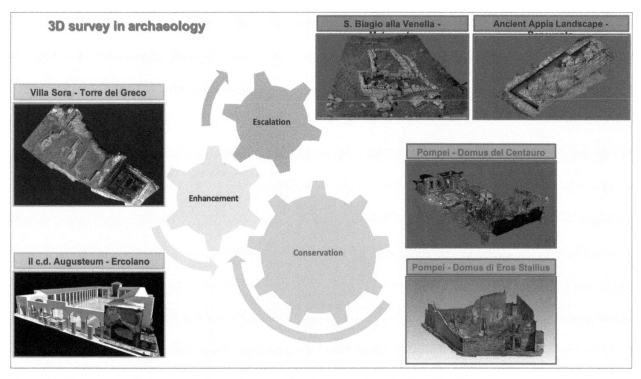

Figure 74. 3D survey applied to excavation, enhancement and conversation of cultural heritage.

Three-dimensional documentation of the entire site based different techniques (laser scanner, terrestrial and aerial photogrammetry) allows to obtain an accurate survey of the actual situation – this is useful to the correct re-interpretation of the previous documentation and to the planning of the new excavation. The large-scale survey with laser scanner and photogrammetric survey by means of a drone, allow an assessment of the morphological context in which the structures are placed. Instead, a detailed survey with terrestrial photogrammetry allows to fill the missing data of the old excavation documentation and to manage in an efficient and expeditious manner the information from the new digs.

In the case study of the Ancient Appia Landscapes, the three-dimensional documentation of the ongoing excavation makes it possible to obtain high-resolution DEM, contour lines and ortho-photos in a timely manner while also minimizing costs and expeditious manner. In addition, these can be integrated into the GIS management system of the research data. This information, crossed with the data of ancient cartography and with those coming from geophysical investigations, prove valuable to the interpretation of the archaeological context.

The cases therefore show that the 3D surveys obtained with the SfM technique, linked (and then scaled and georeferenced) to topographic polygons (obtained with GPS or Total Station) allow to have a level of precision that enables extraction of a very large amount of information. The high-resolution photorealistic quality allows to have ortho-photos from which it is possible to produce the traditional vector documentation, which in turn allows an

objective characterization, free of the approximations due to the reduced time to acquire on field data.

Software have been developed that allow to automatically extract profiles from the 3D model. This, in turn, allows to have plans and sections of the excavation area if needed – even ex-post (i.e., even for late study). Secant section planes can be set at centimetres distance, allowing a very large documentation detail, without being constrained by the pegs placed during the excavation, and perfectly faithful to reality.

The innovative survey procedures therefore allow an optimization of the on-field activities making these not only faster and more precise but also less resource intensive as they require less staff.

On the other hand, we note that such methodologies, require more processing and computational power – the process can take even a few hours only for the alignment phase. This will result in a higher level of unpredictability – as far as the timing is concerned. This may not always be compatible with the timing of an excavation in progress. Therefore, adequate planning of the relevant operations is necessary to prevent the risk of accidental loss of information (Figure 75 and Figure 76).

6.2 Survey for redevelopment and enhancement

The archaeological site of Villa Sora in Torre del Greco is located in an extremely difficult and problematic surrounding which makes the site unknown and inaccessible to the general public. These situations require

PHOTOGRAMMETRIC 3D SURVEY FOR ARCHAEOLOGY

ADVANTAGES	DISADVANTAGES
• faithfully return of the excavation • elimination of subjectivity in the planimetric representation • acquisition speed • measurability of the excavation in the three dimensions (X,Y,Z) • integration of 3D and 2D information • geo-referencing the survey • easy interpretation • completeness of the survey	• atmospheric conditioning for colour rendering • processing not always contemporaneous to the excavation • long processing times in case of complex datasets

Figure 75. Summary of the advantages and disadvantages of using 3D survey by photogrammetry for archaeological excavations.

LASER SCANNING SURVEY FOR ARCHAEOLOGY

ADVANTAGES	DISADVANTAGES
• faithful metric restitution in three dimensions • Removal of subjectivity in the planimetric representation • acquisition speed • Integrated, and easy to set, positioning and calibration sensors • geo-referencing the survey • acquisition of RGB data	• long processing times • software often lacking in intuition. • low photographic resolution • heavy and complex files to manage

Figure 76. Summary of the advantages and disadvantages found in the use of 3D survey using Laser Scanner tools for archaeological excavation.

an intervention that aims to redevelop and enhance the archaeological site. This is done through designing a restoration project that allows for its use and, consequently, inserts the site into a tourist path.

The model obtained through the laser scanner survey allows for the updating of the existing planimetry and provides an overview of the archaeological remains. This serves to virtually eliminate visual "barriers". In fact, the area is distinct from areas covered by the preservation of decorated environment, or without protection. This does not allow for the real perception of the original floor elevations.

Again, the complete vision of the digital excavations allows us to extract plans that can be compared with the historical planimetry and possibly make new interpretations of the villa's rooms. In addition, the detailed survey with

the image-based methodology allows us to obtain high resolution models and, therefore, high definition ortho-photos of the walls of the different environments. This serves as to document the state of conservation of the paintings and wall structures and obtain the necessary supports for the analysis of structural and painted surfaces degradation. This follows the example of what was done in the context of the Great Pompeii Project.

There is no valorisation without maintenance. The accurate 3D survey provides support for adequate planning of the restorations, for the installation of a new roof and an adequate visit path. Not least, the models obtained can be reused as a basis for designing a virtual, navigable model suitable for visitors.

Even the work on the so-called *Augusteum* of Ercolano starts from a detailed analysis of the historical plans and previous research to obtain as much detailed information on a structure that is for the most part inaccessible as it is submerged in volcanic debris. What is presented to the visitor is only part of the facade, mainly the four-faced arch, a south corner of the large portico that characterizes the building.

The intervention shows how in these situations it is possible to couple the acquisitions that follow the terrestrial photogrammetry technique with the data of the total station. This allows for the reconstruction and virtually placement of the structure in space. In this way it is possible to read and understand the building in its entirety, on one's own computer, from the scarce real data available (in this case the arch).

It also shows how it is possible to add, in the final virtual model, digital copies (obtained with the same photogrammetric technique) of statues, whose origin is given by historical excavation diaries. The model thus obtained can be used with an attached information scheme that also guarantees its scientific reliability and reuse for research purposes online.

6.3 Surveys for conservation and preventive maintenance

The 'built archaeology' case study clearly demonstrates that the optimal solution for the definition and implementation of maintenance and conservation procedures of ancient monuments is obtained through the synergistic action between the archaeological, architectural and engineering skills.

In this context, the figure of the archaeologist, expert in the analysis of ancient buildings and construction techniques, can be a functional added value to the careful study of monuments. Surveys are the essential tool to extract the possible cultural context meanings and thus become a primary source of information.

The Pompeian case study allowed us to test, in complex archaeological area, expeditious 3D survey methodologies, for the purpose of studying and maintaining the structures.

In the case study of Eros Stallius, the primary objectives of the investigations are to provide detailed support for archaeological research and allow for the maintenance of the structures through a low-cost three-dimensional investigation. The use and integration of the results obtained with the use of three methodologies (traditional topography, terrestrial photogrammetry and aerial photogrammetry) allows to highlight the advantages and limitations of each technique.

Indeed, the absence of stratigraphic information inherent to the site makes paramount the correct reading of vertical stratigraphy, as is the only source of information on the life of the structure. The significant heights of some of the walls, however, do not allow for the total coverage of the surfaces using only the terrestrial photogrammetry.

In order not to get away from the low-cost spirit of the project, a drone that does not have the ability to plan the flight path in advance, but is modified ad hoc with a photographic sensor of better quality than the standard one expected, can be used to acquire images at higher altitude. Thanks to the topographical references arranged in the acquisition phase with these two techniques, two metric valid models can be obtained. These models will serve different aspects relating to the knowledge of the site.

Therefore, it is evident that the integration of different techniques is particularly useful for the survey of high structures. This integration not only solves visibility problems but can improve the definition and measurement of the vertical and horizontal planes of the walls. This will reduce any distortion.

In addition, when access to the site is prohibited, we can take advantage of a valid metric three-dimensional copy of the structure, which is fundamental to the continuation of the investigations on the vertical stratigraphies.

The study of the *Casa del Centauro* is linked to a large project that over the years has deepened the knowledge of the oldest phases of the domus, but is part of a planning phase for the safety of the structures of the *Regio* VI. The objective of the three-dimensional survey of the rooms set on the proto-house was to define a 3D digital replica of the state of affairs from which information could be extracted at any time (plans and sections, heights, ortho-photos, dimensions, etc.). This would allow us the possibility of obtaining models with different resolution for the analysis of structural and surface degradation, as well as for didactic research (mainly the completion of the elevated analysis) or fruition research.

The activity shows that the high accuracy of the 3D relief allows for ease monitoring of the state of the structures and provides one with the possibility of repeating the acquisitions over time. In fact, by inserting the same GCPs, it is possible to proceed with a direct comparison of the models obtained at different times. This will allow us to identify any misalignments or failures. The ortho-photos extracted from the 3D model are also correct in all their planes, allowing accurate measurement of niches, windows and altars. This is not possible with common photo- straightening.

However, given the complexity of acquiring some elements (such as columns) it is essential to integrate multiple survey techniques (terrestrial photogrammetry, laser scanner and total station).

6.4 Final thoughts and future developments

The "traditional" survey methodologies have always provided archaeology with information relevant to the different phases of research. Plans, sections and altitudes, also acquired with sophisticated instruments, such as the total station or GPS systems, crossed with photographic data and detail cards, are still archaeologist´s daily working tools. However, these procedures usually lack the detail required by the procedures relevant to the conservation and enhancement of heritage goods. This is because an objective detailed documentation with traditional methods requires time investment (and thus money) which is not generally sustainable in ordinary projects. The historian's work in the field is consequently detached from the process that involves the survival and dissemination of understanding heritage.

The collapses in Pompeii have brought to public attention the need to integrate scheduled maintenance processes into research. The figure of the archaeologist is that of an indispensable actor, both regarding these processes as well as in the redevelopment of "forgotten" archaeological areas. It is therefore the task of correct archaeological documentation to take into account all these aspects of research, enhancement and conservation.

The innovative three-dimensional survey methodologies fit perfectly into the growing need for information of the highest quality and detail that fills the shortcomings of traditional topographic surveying whilst integrating the collection of different kinds of information through increasingly automated shipping systems.

Whatever the chosen technique to operate the survey (terrestrial or aerial image-based, range-based) the result will be a digital replica of reality, that can be employed and questioned 'on demand' now or in the future to study (Figure 77) archaeological heritage, its enhancement and conservation.

In this way, large-scale dissemination becomes a part of the process of enhancing the archaeological heritage, no longer the main purpose of the three-dimensional survey. A correct set of metadata – specially created for three-dimensional measurements – can be reuse after a long time, facilitating new study actions. Much more complex, if not impossible, is the reconstitution of an asset on the basis of data that have been obtained for a generally subjective and non-replicable selection process, since the beginning of the survey, through "traditional" techniques.

In the field of archaeological research on site, the constant computer updates and developments in terms of technologies and tools for three-dimensional surveying allow us to finally propose a project to develop a 3D documentation of stratigraphic excavation.

Obviously, the management of a three-dimensional survey accompanied by a huge amount of data, often

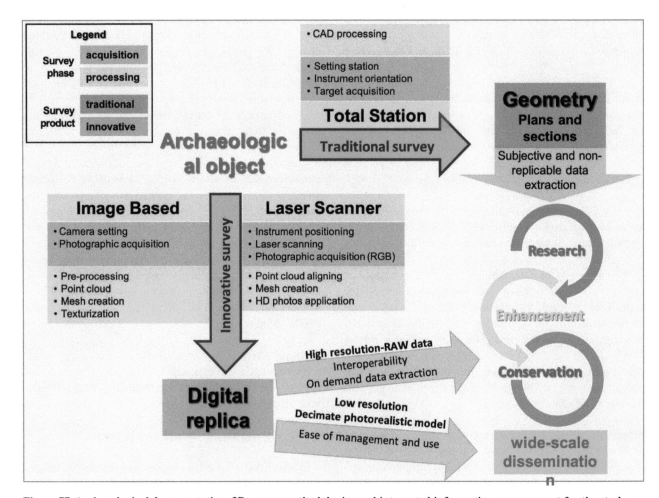

Figure 77. Archaeological documentation: 3D survey methodologies and integrated information management for the study, conservation and enhancement of archaeological heritage.

heterogeneous, requires an adequate storage system, in order to make proper use of the information.

In this regard, it has been shown that integrated approaches (such as BIM) make it possible to manage heterogeneous information (including 3D) usable in multidisciplinary areas. This also allows for the exploitation of data in its entirety, guaranteeing its integrity, thanks to the use of exchange formats standard (IFC). However, it has also been shown that BIM requires a level of knowledge of non-elementary support., which is less intuitive.

The systematic use of these techniques is held back by the still too complicated way of extracting some information from 3D. Basic operations (such as the extraction of plans and sections) often require the passage of multiple software, some of which are necessary to only obtain the file extension readable by the final program. In this sense, it is appropriate to develop software dedicated to archaeological problems that avoid innumerable and useless data passages.

Furthermore, there is an evident need for an archaeologist figure who has minimum basic knowledge of these technologies and above all a clear methodological approach to use it for research purposes.

To fulfil this purpose, it is necessary to build on current traditional technique and establish guidelines and manuals on: 3D surveys methodologies, integrated management of information and the conservation and enhancement of archaeological heritage.

References

Achille C., Fassi F., Mandelli A., Moerlin B. 2014 "The yards of the Milan Cathedral: tradition and BIM" In *Proceedings of the international conference preventive and planned conservation Monza*, Mantua, 5–9 May 2014, pp. 147-156.

Adamesteanu D. 1964, "La documentazione archeologica in Basilicata", *Atti del IV Convegno di Studi sulla Magna Grecia*, Taranto 1964 (Napoli 1965), pp.121-143.

Adamesteanu D. 1973, "L'attività archeologica in Basilicata", *Atti del XIII Convegno di Studi sulla Magna Grecia*, Taranto 1973 (Napoli 1974), 442-456.

Adembri, B. Alonso-Durá, A. Juan-Vidal, F. Bertacchi, G. Bertacchi, S. Cipriani, L. Fantini, F. Soriano-Estevalis, B. 2016. "Modelli digitali 3D per documentare, conoscere ed analizzare l'architettura e la costruzione nel mondo antico: l'esempio della Sala Ottagonale delle Piccole Terme di Villa Adriana". *Archeologia e Calcolatori*, 27. pp. 291-316. ISSN 1120-6861

Allison P. M. 2004. "Pompeian Households: An On-line Companion is a publication of The Stoa: A Consortium for Electronic Publication in the Humanities", Ross Scaife, ed. http://www.stoa.org/projects/ph/house?id=5

Allroggen-Bedel A. 2010, "A proposito dei Balbi: note archivistiche alla topografia d'Ercolano", in C. Gasparri, G. Greco, R. Pierobon Benoit (eds.), *Dall'immagine alla storia. Studi per ricordare Stefania Adamo Muscettola, Quaderni del Centro Studi Magna Grecia* 10, Napoli, Naus, 355-373.

Allroggen-Bedel A. 2008, "L'Augusteum", in M.P. Guidobaldi (ed.), *Ercolano. Tre secoli di scoperte.* Catalogo della Mostra (Napoli 2009), Milano, Electa, 35-45.

Amici C.M. 2008. "Survey and technical analysis: a must for understanding ancient monuments" in *ARCHAIA: Case Studies on Research, Planning, Characterisation, Conservation and Management of Archaeological Sites*, BAR S1877, Oxford 2008, pp. 29-41.

Arnold, D. 1991, *Building in Egypt. Pharaonic Stone Masonry*. Oxford – New York.

Berggren Å., Dell'Unto N. Forte M., Haddow S., Hodder I., Issavi J., Lercari N., Mazzuccato C., Mickel A., Taylor J. 2015. "Revisiting reflexive archaeology at Çatalhöyük: integrating digital and 3D technologies at the trowel's edge". In: *Antiquity*, Vol. 89, No. 344, 2015, p. 433-448.

Bezzi A., Bezzi L., Ducke B. 2010. "Computer Vision e Structure From Motion, nuove metodologie per la documentazione archeological tridimensionale: un approccio aperto" in *ArcheoFOSS. Open Source, Free Software e Open Format nei processi di ricerca archeologici*. Foggia. Volume 5.

Bew, M.; Richards, M. Bew-Richards BIM Maturity Model. 2008.

Bianchini, C., Nicastro, S. 2018. "From BIM to H-BIM". *2018 3rd Digital Heritage International Congress (DigitalHERITAGE) Held Jointly with 2018 24th International Conference on Virtual Systems & Multimedia (VSMM 2018)*.

Bitelli G. 2002, "Moderne tecniche e strumentazioni per il rilievo dei beni culturali", *atti del Convegno nazionale ASITA*, 2002.

Bitelli G., Tini M.A., Vittuari L. 2003. "Low-height aerial photogrammetry for archaeological orthoimaging production". *ISPRS Archives Vol. XXXIV, Part 5/W12*, pp. 55-59.

Bitelli, G., Dellapasqua, M., Girelli, V.A., Sanchini E., Tini, M.A. 2017. "3D Geomatic techniques for an integrated approach to Cultural Heritage knowledge: the case of San Michele in. Acerboli's Church in Sant'Arcangelo di Romagna. Int. Arch. Photogramm. Remote Sens. Spatial Inf. Sci., XLII-5-W1, 291

Borchardt, L. 1905, *Das Re-Heiligtum des Königs Ne-Woser-Re, I Bd. Der Bau (hrsg. von F.W. von Bissing)*. Berlin.

Borchardt, L. 1907, "Das Grabdenkmal des Königs Ne-user-Re' (Ausgrabungen der Deutschen Orient-Gesellschaft" *in Abusir 1902-1904 – I Bd.)*. Leipzig.

Borchardt, L. 1909, "Das Grabdenkmal des Königs Nefer-ir-ka-Re' (Ausgrabungen der Deutschen Orient – Gesellschaft" *in Abusir 1902-1908 – V Bd.)*. Leipzig.

Bornaz L., Dequal S., Lingua A. 2006. "L'ortofoto solida di precisione: un prodotto innovativo per la rappresentazione e la gestione dei dati tridimensionali". *Atti Conferenza nazionale SIFET*, Taranto.

Bosco A., Barbarino M., Valentini R., D'Andrea A. 2015a. "Low-cost surveys of the Domus of Stallius Eros in Pompeii" in *ISPRS Archives*, vol. XL, part. 5/W4. p. 187-192, doi: 10.5194/isprsarchives-XL-5-W4-187-2015.

Bosco A., Barbarino M., Valentini R., D'Andrea A. 2015b. "Pompeii, Domus di Stallius Eros: comparison between terrestrial and aerial low-cost surveys". In *43rd International Conference on Computer Applications and Quantitative Methods in Archaeology (CAA)*. Siena 2015.

Bosco A., D'Andrea A., Nuzzolo M., Pirelli R., Zanfagna P., 2018. "A virtual reconstruction of the sun temple of Niuserra: from scans to BIM". In *44th International Conference on Computer Applications and Quantitative Methods in Archaeology* (CAA). Oslo 2016.

Bosco A., D'andrea A., Nuzzolo M., Zanfagna P., 2019, "A BIM approach for the analysis of an archaeological monument", in *International Archives of the Photogrammetry, Remote Sensing and Spatial Information Sciences*, vol. XLII-2/W9, p. 165-172

Bosco A., Carpentiero L., D'Andrea A., Minucci E., Valentini R., 2020. "A drone survey to support an archaeological BIM: the project at Insula 4-6 of Paestum". *D-SITE, Drones – Systems of Information on culTural hEritage. For a spatial and social investigation.* Salvatore Barba, Sandro Parrinello, Marco Limongiello, Anna Dell'Amico (edited by) – Pavia: Pavia University Press, 2020. ISBN 978-88-6952-120-1 ISBN 978-88-6952-129-4 OA.

Brienza E., Gabrielli R., Artegiani L. 2014, "Roma, Metro C: il GIS per la gestione della documentazione 3D degli scavi stratigrafici preventivi", in *atti della 15a Conferenza Utenti Esri 2014, Roma, 9 – 10 Aprile 2014, in GEOMEDIA, Supplemento al* n° 2-2014, pp. 1-8, ESRI Italia, ISSN: 1128-8132.

Brienza E., Carlani R. 2015, "Information and Communication Technology per la ricostruzione virtuale delle architetture e dei paesaggi antichi finalizzata alla valorizzazione e al restauro", in *atti del Convegno Nazionale di Geoarcheologia. La geoarcheologia come chiave di lettura per uno sviluppo sostenibile del territorio*, 4-5 Luglio 2014, Aidone (EN)

Brumana R., Georgopolous A., Oreni D., Raimondi A., Bregianni A. 2013, "HBIM for documentation, dissemination and management of Built Heritage. The case study of St. Maria in Scaria d'Intelvi", in *International Journal of Heritage in the Digital Era*, Vol. 2, n. 3, pp. 434-451.

Buscemi, F., Militello, P., D'Agostino, G., Sammito, A.M. 2014. "Tecniche di fotomodellazione per la documentazione e la comunicazione in archeologia: il sito di Calicantone (RG)." In *Archeologia e Calcolatori n. XXV – 2014.* pp. 131-156

Campana S., Francovich R. 2007, "Sistemi informativi territoriali per i beni culturali della Toscana. Strategie, metodi e tecnologie per l'analisi, la gestione e il monitoraggio del territorio" in M. Guaitoli (a cura di), *Sistemi informativi territoriali per i beni culturali del territorio*, Atti del Convegno (Roma, 31 gennaio 2006). 17 pp.

Campana S., Remondino F. 2008. "Fast and Detailed Digital Documentation of Archaeological Excavations and Heritage Artifacts. Layers of Perception". 35th *Proceedings of the CAA Conference (Dr. Rudolf Habelt GmbH, Bonn)*, pp. 36-42.

Carpentiero L. 2018. "La metodologia BIM (Building Information Modelling) per l'acquisizione, l'elaborazione e l'integrazione dei dati di rilievo per lo studio, la conservazione e la valorizzazione del costruito storico" in *Newsletter di Archeologia CISA*, Volume 9, 2018, pp. 1-21

Cecchi R., Gasparoli P. 2010. *Prevenzione e manutenzione per i Beni Culturali edificati. Procedimenti scientifici per lo sviluppo delle attività ispettive. Il caso studio delle aree archeologiche di Roma e Ostia Antica*, Alinea, Firenze, 2010, pp. 334 – (ISBN 978-88-6055-576-2).

Chiabrando F., Costamagna E., Rinaudo F., Spanò A. 2010. "Very close nadiral images: a proposal for quick digging survey", *International Archives of Photogrammetry, Remote Sensing and Spatial Information Sciences*, Vol. XXXVIII, Part 5 Commission V Symposium, Newcastle upon Tyne, UK. 2010.

Chiabrando F., Lingua A., Maschio P., Rinaudo F., Spanò A. 2012. "Mezzi aerei non convenzionali a volo autonomo per il rilievo fotogrammetrico in ambito archeologico". In: *Una giornata informale per i 70 anni del Prof. Carlo Monti – 3 Maggio 2012*, Milano, 3 maggio 2012. pp. 1-12

Chiabrando F, Sammartano G., Spanò A. 2016, "Historical Buildings Models and their handling via 3D survey: from point clouds to user-oriented HBIM" *In Arch. Photogramm. Remote Sens. Spatial Inf. Sci.*, XLI-B5, pp. 633-640.

Cinquantaquattro T. E. 2016, "Attività della Soprintendenza 'archeologia' della Basilicata" in *Atti del LXVI Convegno di Studi sulla Magna Grecia*, Taranto 2016, c.d.s.

Cinquantaquattro T. E. 2011, "monitoraggio, carta del rischio archeologico e programmazione", in Cecchi: *Roma archeologia. Interventi per la tutela e la fruizione del patrimonio archeologico*. III Rapporto, Electa, Milano.

Clemen, C., 2022, "Trends in BIM And GIS Standardization – Report from the Joint ISO/TC59/SC13–ISO/TC211 WG: GIS-BIM". In *Int. Arch. Photogramm. Remote Sens. Spatial Inf. Sci.*, XLVI-5/W1-2022, 51–58, https://doi.org/10.5194/isprs-archives-XLVI-5-W1-2022-51-2022

Court S., Thompson J., Guidobaldi M.P. 2011. "L'esperienza dell'Herculaneum Conservation Project, un progetto pubblico-privato per la conservazione degli Scavi di Ercolano". In Buondonno, E., Biggi, C. & Battisti, E. (eds) *Progetti di architettura. Concorsi, realizzazioni e sperimentazioni*. Atti. Napoli, Doppiavoce: 27-35.

D'Andrea A. 2008, "Sharing 3D Archaeological Data: Tools and Semantic Approaches", in *14th International Conference on Virtual Systems and Multimedia, Limassol*, Cyprus, October 20th – 25th, 2008.

D'Andrea A. 2011, "Il rilievo archeologico con il laser scanner: luci e ombre", in *Vesuviana, An International Journal of Archaeological and Historical Studies on Pompeii and Hercolaneum*, 3, 193-218.

D'Andrea A., Barbarino M. 2012, "Modellare lo scavo archeologico: esperienze e tecniche a confront", in *Archeologia e Calcolatori* n. XXIII, p. 229-245.

D'Andrea A. 2013. "Provenance and Paradata in Open Data: 3D-ICONS model" *MapPapers 1-III,* 2013, pp.1-86 doi:10.4456/MAPPA.2013.17.

D'Andrea A., Fernie K. 2013, "3D-ICONS metadata schema for 3D objects", *Newsletter di Archeologia CISA 4*, pp. 159-181.

D'Andrea A., Pirelli R., Iannone G., Nuzzolo M., Zanfagna P. 2014, "The Italian Archaeological Mission in the The Sun Temple of Niuserra at Abu Ghurab, Egypt. The Use of Combined Technologies and New Perspectives of Study on the Monument: the two First Campaigns", in N*ewsletter di Archeologia CISA*, Volume (5), pp. 58-98.

D'Andrea A., Bosco A., Barbarino M. 2017. "A 3D environment to rebuild virtually the so-called Augusteum in Herculaneum" in *Archeologia e Calcolatori – Proceedings of the KAINUA 2017 International Conference in Honour of Professor Giuseppe Sassatelli's 70th Birthday* (Bologna, 18-21 April 2017), 28.2, 2017, 437-446.

Dell'Unto, N., Landeschi, G., 2022. Archaeological 3D GIS (1st ed.). Routledge. https://doi. org/10.4324/9781003034131

De Luca L., Bussayarat C., Stefani C., Veron P., Florenzano M. 2011, "A semantic-based platform for the digital analysis of architectural heritage", *Computers & Graphics*, 2011, 35(2), 227-241.

De Stefano F. 2014, "Il repertorio iconografico del santuario di S. Biagio alla Venella (Metaponto) all'alba della colonia", in *Antesteria* 3, 157-169.

De Stefano F. 2016, "Ricomporre e interpretare l'antico. Un caso di studio dal santuario metapontino di San Biagio alla Venella", in *Dialoghi sull'Archeologia della Magna Grecia e del Mediterraneo*, Fondazione Paestum, 7-9 settembre 2016), c.s.

De Vita C. B., Terribile A. 2016. "The Landscapes of the Ancient Appia Project: Formation and Degeneration Processes in Landscapes Stratification of the Benevento Area", LAC 2014 *Proceedings 3rd International Landscape Archaeology Conference*. DOI 10.5463/lac.2014.14

Dell'Unto N., Leander A. M., Ferdani D., Dellepiane M., Callieri M., Lindgren S. 2013. "Digital reconstruction and visualisation in archaeology: case-study drawn from the work of the Swedish Pompeii Project*". Digital Heritage International Congress* pp.621-628.

Demetrescu E., 2018. "Virtual Reconstruction as a Scientific Tool: The Extended Matrix and Source-Based Modelling Approach." In *Digital Research and Education in Architectural Heritage*, 102–116.

Dessales H., Ponce J., Letellier É., Marchand- Beaulieu F., Monier F., Péron A., Ubelmann Y. 2014. "Pompéi. Villa de Diomède", *Chronique des activités archéologiques de l'École française de Rome [En ligne], Les cités vésuviennes*, 06 mars 2014

Di Benedetto M., Ponchio F., Ganovelli F., Scopigno R. 2010. "Spidergl: a javascript 3d graphics library for next-generation WWW". New York, NY, USA, ACM, pp. 165-174.

Doerr M., Theodoridou M. 2011, "CRMdig: A generic digital provenance model for scientific observation", in *Proceedings of TaPP 2011: 3rd USENIX Workshop on the Theory and Practice of Provenance*, Heraklion, Greece. June 2011.

Dore C., Murphy M., McCarthy S., Brechin F., Casidy C., Dirix E. 2015, "Structural Simulations and Conservation Analysis -Historic Building Information Model (HBIM)", *In. Arch. Photogramm. Remote Sens. Spatial Inf. Sci.*, XL-5/W4, pp. 351-357.

Ducke B. 2012. "Natives of a connected world: free and open source software in archaeology". *World Archaeology* 44:4 pp.571-579.

Eastman C. et al. 2008. *BIM Handbook: A Guide to Building Information Modeling for Owners, Managers, Designers, Engineers and Contractors*, John Wiley and Sons, NY, 2008.

Eisenbeiss, H., Lambers, K., Sauerbier, M., Zhang, L. 2005. "Photogrammetric documentation of an archaeological site (Palpa, Peru) using an autonomous model helicopter". *ISPRS Archives Vol. XXXIV-5/C34, CIPA*, Torino, Italy, pp. 238-243.

El-Hakim SF., Beraldin JA., Picard M., Godin G. 2004. "Detailed 3D reconstruction of large-scale heritage sites with integrated techniques", *IEEE Computer Graphics and Applications*, 2004, pp. 21-29.

Fichera, M.G., Malnati, L., Mancinelli, M.L. 2015. "Grande Progetto Pompei: la Direzione Generale per le Antichità e il piano della conoscenza" in Archeologia e Calcolatori, Supplemento 7 – 2015. II SITAR nella Rete della ricerca italiana. Verso la conoscenza archeologica condivisa. Atti del III Convegno (Roma, Museo Nazionale Romano, 23-24 maggio 2013)

Fiorini A. 2013. "nuove possibilità della fotogrammetria. La documentazione archeologica del nuraghe di Tanca Manna (Nuoro)", *Archeologia e Calcolatori n. XXIV –* 2013. pp. 341-354

Fiorini A. 2012. "Tablet pc, fotogrammetria e pdf 3d: strumenti per documentare l'archeologia". In *Archeologia e calcolatori*, 23, 2012, pp. 213-227.

Fiorini A., Archetti V. 2011. "Fotomodellazione e stereofotogrammetria per la creazione di modelli stratigrafici in archeologia dell'architettura", in *Archeologia e Calcolatori*, 2011, XXII, pp. 199 – 216

Forte M., Danelon N., Biancifiori E, Dell'Unto N., Lercari N. 2015. "Building 89 and 3D Digging Project" In Çatalhöyük *2015 Archive Report* p.215-247-

Forte M. 2014, "3D archaeology: New perspectives and challenges – The example of Catalhyük", *Journal of Eastern Mediterranean Archaeology and Heritage Studies*, 2, 1, 1-29.

Garagnani S., Gaucci, A., Govi, E. 2016, "ArchaeoBIM: dallo scavo al Building Information Modeling di una struttura sepolta. Il caso del tempio tuscanico di Uni a Marzabotto", in *Archeologia e Calcolatori* n. XXVII, pp. 251-270.

Garagnani S. 2017, Archaeological Building Information Modeling: beyond scalable representation of architecture and archaeology, *Archeologia e Calcolatori* n. XXVIII.2, pp. 141-149.

Garagnani S., Gaucci A., Moscati P., Gaini M., 2021. *ArcheoBIM. Theory, Processes and Digital Methodologies for the Lost Heritage*. Bononia University Press, 2021.

Giardino L. 2012, "Aree urbane e territori della costa ionica della Basilicata tra Pirro e Annibale", *Atti del LII Convegno di Studi sulla Magna Grecia*, Taranto 2012, Taranto 2015, 573-617.

Grell, C. 1982. *Herculanum et Pompéi dans les récits des voyageurs français du xviiie siècle*. Publications du Centre Jean Bérard. doi :10.4000/books.pcjb.233

Guidi G. 2014, "Terrestrial optical active sensors – Theory and applications", in *3D recording and modelling in archaeology and cultural heritage*, BAR International Series, 2014, pp. 37-60.

Guidi G., Remondino F., Russo M., Menna F., Rizzi A., Ercoli S. 2009, "A multi-resolution methodology for the 3D modeling of large and complex archeological areas", in *International Journal of Architectural Computing*, 7 (1), pp. 39-55.

Guidi G., Beraldin J.-A., Ciofi S., Atzeni C. 2003. "Fusion of range camera and photogrammetry: A systematic procedure for improving 3-D models metric accuracy", *Transactions on Systems, Man, and Cybernetics*, Part B, 33(4), pp. 667–676.

Guidobaldi M.P. 2016. "Qualche riflessione sull'esperienza dell'Herculaneum Conservation Project". In Bonetto J., Busana M.S., Giotto A.R., Salvadori M., Zanovello P. (eds) *I mille volti del passato. Scritti in onore di Francesca Ghedini*. Roma: Edizioni Quasar.

Guidobaldi M. P. 2015, "Villa Breglia e Villa Sora di Torre del Greco: problemi e prospettive", in *Newsletter di Archeologia CISA*, Volume 6, 2015, 107-12

Guidobaldi M.P. 2012, "Un edificio del culto imperiale a Ercolano", in S. De Caro (ed.), *Antichità da Ercolano. Catalogo della Mostra* (St. Petersburg 2011-2012), San Pietroburgo, MondoMostre, 31-42.

Kott K. 2012. "Digital repository best practices for cultural heritage organizations". *Computer History Museum*, February 3, 2012

Laino A., Massari A., Pesaresi P. 2014. "La manutenzione programmata ad Ercolano; obiettivi e complessità di una macchina di cura continua e sostenibile" in *Estratti del 30° Convegno di Studi SCIENZA E BENI CULTURALI* Bressanone 1 - 4 luglio 2014. ISSN 2039-9790 ISBN 978-88-95409-18-4

Langella A., 1978. Antiche strutture romane: *Villa Sora: reportage archeologico [del] Gruppo Archeologico Napoletano [di] Torre del Greco*. Pubblicazione a cura della Sezione Torrese del Gruppo Archeologico Napoletano. A. C. M., 1978.

Lercari, N., Shiferaw, E., Forte, M., Kopper, R. 2017. "Immersive Visualization and Curation of Archaeological Heritage Data: Çatalhöyük and the Dig@IT App". *Journal of Archaeological Method and Theory* (2017). DOI: 10.1007/s10816-017-9340-4.

Lerma García, J.L., Van Genechten B., Santana Quintero M., 2008, *3D Risk Mapping. Theory and Practice on Terrestrial Laser Scanning. Training Material Based on Practical Applications*. Universidad Politécnica de Valencia, Valencia 2008, 261 pp.

Licheri A. 2016. "Prospettive sull'utilizzo del Building Information Modelling (BIM) in archeologia" in *Archeologia e Calcolatori, Supplemento 8, 2016, 197-202*

Lopez, F. J., Lerones, P. M., Llamas, J., Bermejo Gòmez-Garcìa, J., Zalama, E. 2018, "A Review of Heritage Building Information Modeling (H-BIM)", *Multimodal Technologies Interact,* 2(2), 21, pp. 1-29.

Maiuri, A. 1929. Pompei – Relazione sui lavori di scavo dall'aprile 1926 al dicembre 1927. In *Notizie degli Scavi di Antichità*, Serie 6, n. 5, pp. 354-476.

Manacorda D. 2004. *Prima lezione di archeologia*. Ed. Laterza. Roma-Bari 2004.

Mastursi L. 2008, "Modello ricostruttivo della cd. Basilica di Ercolano", in R. Cantilena, A. Porzio (eds.), *Herculanense Museum. Laboratorio sull'antico nella Reggia di Portici*, Napoli, Electa, 314-319.

Matrone, F., Colucci, E., De Ruvo, V., Lingua, A., & Spanò, A. 2019. "HBIM in a semantic 3D GIS database", in *Int. Arch. Photogramm. Remote Sens. Spatial Inf. Sci.*, XLII-2/W11, 857–865, https://doi.org/10.5194/isprs-archives-XLII-2-W11-857-2019

Medri M. 2003, *Manuale di rilievo archeologico*. BARI, Laterza.

Mickel A. 2015. "Reasons for Redundancy in Reflexivity: The Role of Diaries in Archaeological Epistemology." *Journal of Field Archaeology* 40 (3): 300–309.

Morgan C., Wright H. 2018, "Pencils and Pixels: Drawing and Digital Media" in *Archaeological Field Recording. Journal of Field Archaeology*, 1–16.

Murphy M., McGovern E., Pavia S. 2009, "Historic building information modelling (HBIM)", in *Structural Survey* Vol. 27 (Issue: 4): 311 – 327.

Murphy M., McGovern E., Pavia S. 2011, "Historic Building Information Modelling – Adding intelligence to laser and image-based surveys", *Int. Arch. Photogramm. Remote Sens. Spatial Inf. Sci.*, XXXVIII-5/W16, pp. 1-7.

Murphy M. 2012, *Historic Building Information Modelling (HBIM) For Recording and Documenting Classical Architecture in Dublin 1700 to 1830*. Dublin 2012

Najbjerg T. 2002, "A reconstruction and reconsideration of the so-called basilica", in T. McGinn, P. Carafa, N. de Grummond, B. Bergmann, T. Najbjerg (eds.), *Pompeian Brothels, Pompeii's Ancient History, Mirrors and Mysteries, Art and Nature at Oplontis, and the Herculaneum "Basilica", Journal of Roman Archaeology*, Supplementary Series 47, 122-165.

Nava M.L. 1999, "L'attività archeologica in Basilicata nel 1998", in *Magna Grecia e Oriente mediterraneo prima dell'età ellenistica, Atti del XXXIX Convegno di Studi sulla Magna Grecia*, Taranto (1999), Napoli 2000, pp. 689 ss.

NBIMS, *National BIM-standard-United States* (https://www.nationalbimstandard.org), accessed: 7 April 2022.

Nex F., Remondino F. 2014. "UAV for 3D mapping applications: a review" in *Applied geomatics, 2014*. Pp. 1-15. ISSN: 1866-928X

Novaković P., Hornak M., Zachar M., Joncic N., 2017. *3D Digital Recording of Archaeological, Architectural and Artistic Heritage*. CONPRA Series, Vol. I. 10.4312/9789612378981.

Nuzzolo M. 2010. "I Templi Solari e l'Ideologia Regale nell'Antico Regno". Ph.D. dissertation, Università degli studi di Napoli "L'Orientale", Naples 2010 (in press.)

Nuzzolo, M., Pirelli, R. 2010, "Indagini archeologiche e topografiche nel Tempio solare di Niuserra ad Abu Ghurab", in Pirelli, R. (ed.) *Ricerche Italiane e Scavi in Egitto*, volume (IV), Istituto Italiano di Cultura, Il Cairo, pp. 221-38.

Nuzzolo, M., Pirelli, R. 2011, "New archaeological investigation in the sun temple of Niuserra in Abu Ghurab", in Barta, M., Coppens, F., Krejci, J. (Eds.) *Abusir and Saqqara in the Year 2010*. Proceedings of the Conference held in Prague, May 31st – June 4th, pp. 664-79.

Oreni D., Brumama R., Georgopoulos A., Cuca B. 2014, "HBIM library objects for conservation and management of Built Heritage", in *International Journal of Heritage in the Digital Era*, Vol. 3, n. 2, pp. 321-334.

Ohori, K. A., Biljecki, F., Diakité, A., Krijnen, T., Ledoux, H., & Stoter, J. 2017. TOWARDS AN "Integration of GIS and BIM data: what are the geometric and topological issues?" in *ISPRS Annals of the Photogrammetry, Remote Sensing and Spatial Information Sciences*, 4(4W5), 1–8. https://doi.org/10.5194/isprs-annals-IV-4-W5-1-2017

Osanna M. 2017. "Pompei. Un grande progetto per la conoscenza, la conservazione e la valorizzazione" in Sassatelli G. e Giorgi E. (a cura di) *Pompei intra-extra*. Bononia University Press, 2017.

Pagano M. 1996, "La nuova pianta della città e di alcuni edifici pubblici di Ercolano", in *Cronache Ercolanesi*, 26, 229-257.

Pagano M. 1991, "La villa romana di contrada Sora a Torre del Greco", in *Cronache Ercolanesi*, 21, 149-186, Napoli.

Pavolini C. 2017, Eredità storica e democratica. In cerca di una politica per I Beni Culturali. Ed. Scienze e Lettere, Roma 2017.

Peripimeno M. 2005. "Sperimentazione di tecniche 3D laser scanning per l'analisi e la conservazione del patrimonio archeologico e storico-monumentale. Definizione di procedure e campi di utilizzo". *Convegno Nazionale SIFET 2005*.

Pesando F. 2009. "Case d'età medio-sannitica nella Regio VI di Pompei: periodizzazione degli interventi edilizi e decorative", in La Torre G.F., Torelli M. (a cura di), *Pittura ellenistica in Italia e in Sicilia – Linguaggi e tradizioni* (Messina, 24-25 settembre 2009), Roma, pp. 425-435.

Pesando F., Guidobaldi M.P. 2006, "Pompei, Oplontis, Ercolano, Stabiae". Guide Archeologiche. Laterza, Roma-Bari.

Pesando F. 2003. "Appunti sulla cosiddetta Basilica di Ercolano", *CronErcol 33*, 2003, pp. 331-338.

Piani P. 2013. "La strumentazione UAV nel rilievo e nella modellazione tridimensionale di un sito archeologico" in *Archeomatica*, N° 1 Marzo 2013.

Potenziani M., Callieri M., Dellepiane M., Corsini F., Ponchio R., Scopigno R. 2015 "3DHOP: 3D Heritage Online Presenter". *M. Computers & Graphics* 52, 129-141, 2015.

Prins A. B. 2016. "3D Modeling for Archaeological Documentation: using the JVRP Method to record archaeological excavations with millimeter-accuracy". *JVRP White Papers in Archaeological Technology*. Version 3.0 – September 2016.

Quattrini R., Malinverni E. S., Clini P., Nespeca R., Orlietti E. 2015 "From TLS to HBIM. High quality semantically-aware 3d modeling of complex architecture*", in Arch. Photogramm. Remote Sens. Spatial Inf. Sci.*, XL-5/W4, pp. 367-374.

Reilly, P. 1989. "Data visualisation in archaeology". *IBM systems journal* 28(4) PP.569-579.

Reilly P. 1990. "Towards a virtual archaeology". in: Lockyear K. and Rahtz S. (a cura di) *computer applications in archaeology 1990* PP.133-139.

Remondino, F., El-Hakim S. 2006, "Image-based 3D modelling: a review", in *Photogrammetric Record 21 (115)*, p. 269 – 291.

Remondino F., Girardi, S., Rizzi A., Gonzo, L. 2009, "3D modeling of complex and detailed cultural heritage using multi-resolution data" in *Journal on Computing and Cultural Heritage 2*, 2009, 1, 2:1-2:20.

Remondino F. 2011, "Heritage Recording and 3D Modeling with Photogrammetry and 3D Scanning" *Remote Sens.* 2011, *3*, 1104-1138; doi:10.3390/rs3061104, ISSN 2072-4292

Remondino F., Rizzi A., Agugiaro G., Jimenez B., Menna F.N., Baratti G. 2011, "Rilievi e Modellazione 3D", in *Atti 15° Conferenza Nazionale ASITA*, Reggia di Colorno 15-18 Novembre 2011, 1825-1836

Remondino F., Campana S. 2014, *3D recording and modelling in archaeology and cultural heritage*, BAR International Series, 2014.

Rizzo E., Santoriello A., Capozzoli L., De Martino G., De Vita C. B., Musmeci D., Perciante F. (in press). "Geophysical survey and archaeological data at Masseria Grasso (BN, italy): Ancient Appia Landscapes Project" in *Surveys in Geophysics*.

Santoriello A. 2017. "L'Appia tra Beneventum e ad Calorem: riflessioni e nuovi spunti di ricerca". In *AA.VV. Percorsi. Scritti di Archeologia di e per Angela Pontrandolfo* Pp. 235-252 Paestum, Pandemos. ISBN:978-88-87744-78-1.

Santoriello A. 2017b. "Dalla Convenzione di Faro alle Comunità: raccontare l'archeologia e le vocazioni storiche di un territorio. L'esperienza di Ancient Appia Landscapes" In *Raccontare L'archeologia. Strategie e tecniche per la comunicazione dei risultati delle ricerche archeologiche*. Pp. 103-112. ISBN:978-88-7814-822-2

Santoriello A., Rossi A. 2016. "Un progetto di ricerca tra topografia antica e archeologia dei paesaggi:l'Appia antica nel territorio di Beneventum" in LAC2014 *Proceedings 3rd International Landscape Archaeology Conference*.

Saygi, G., Agugiaro, G., Hamamcioglu-Turan, M., Remondino, F., 2013. "Evaluation of GIS and BIM Roles for the Information Management of Historical Buildings". *ISPRS Ann. Photogramm. Remote Sens. Spatial Inf. Sci.*, Vol. II(5/W1), pp. 283–288.

Saygi G., Remondino F., 2013. "Management of Architectural Heritage Information in BIM and GIS: State of the art and Future Perspectives", in *International Journal of Heritage in the Digital Era*, vol. 2, No 4, 2013, pp. 695-713.

Schilling, S., Clemen, C., 2022. "Practical examples on BIM-GIS integration based on semantic web triplestores". *Int. Arch. Photogramm. Remote Sens. Spatial Inf. Sci.*, XLVI-5/W1, 211-216. https://doi.org/10.5194/isprs-archives-XLVI-5-W1-2022-211-2022

Scianna A. et Al., 2015, "Sperimentazione di tecniche BIM sull'archeologia romana", in *Archeologia e Calcolatori, special issue 7*, pp. 199-212.

Scopigno R., Callieri M., Cignoni P., Corsini M., Dellepiane M., Ponchio F., Ranzuglia G. 2011. "3D models for Cultural Heritage: beyond plain visualization" *IEEE Computer*, Volume 44, Number 7, page 48-55 – July 2011

Sketchfab. 2012. *Sketchfab – The Easiest Way to Share Your 3D Models*. Tratto da https://sketchfab.com/.

Song, Y., Wang, X., Tan, Y., Wu, P., Sutrisna, M., Cheng, J., Hampson, K., 2017. "Trends and Opportunities of BIM-GIS Integration in the Architecture, Engineering and Construction Industry: A Review from a Spatio-Temporal Statistical Perspective". *ISPRS International Journal of Geo-Information*, 6(12), 397. https://doi.org/10.3390/ijgi6120397

Staniforth, S. (ed.) 2013. *Historical Perspectives on Preventive Conservation*. Los Angeles: Getty Conservation Institute.

Tomay L., Santoriello A., Rossi A. 2012. "La via Appia tra tutela e ricerca: recenti indagini di scavo e studi sul territorio beneventano", in Ceraudo G (ed.), *Lungo l'Appia e la Traiana. Le fotografie di Robert Gardner in viaggio con Thomas Ashby nel territorio di Beneventum agli inizi del Novecento*, British School at Rome Archive 10: 19-29. Delta 3, Grottaminarda.

Thompson J., D'Andrea A. 2009. "Gestione di un progetto multidisciplinare in un sito archeologico complesso". In Coralini, A (a c.) *Atti del convegno internazionale "Vesuviana: archeologie a confronto"*. Bologna, 14-16 gennaio 2008. Bologna, Edizioni Antequem: 237-251.

Torelli M. 2004, "La basilica di Ercolano. Una proposta di lettura", *Eidola*, 1, 117-149.

Torelli M. 2011, "Bacchilide, le Pretidi e Artemide *Hemera*a Metaponto. Il culto e la *krene* naomorfa di S. Biagio alla Venella", *Tra protostoria e storia. Studi in onore di Loredana Capuis (Antenor Quaderni 20)*, Roma, 209-221.

Tsiafaki D., Michailidou A., 2015. "Benefits and problems through the application of 3D technologies in archaeology: recording, visualisation, representation and reconstruction", *Scientific Culture 1.3* (2015), 37-45.

Van Balen K. 2015, "Preventive conservation of historic buildings". In *Restoration of Buildings and Monuments Materials science, Conservation of architectural heritage, Sustainable construction.* 21(2–3): 99– 104.

Wheeler, R.E.M. 1923, "Segontium and the Roman Occupation of Wales", *Y Cymmrodor* (The Magazine of the Honourable Society of Cymmrodorion), 33, 1-186.

CPSIA information can be obtained
at www.ICGtesting.com
Printed in the USA
LVHW081656170523
747141LV00008BA/176